America's Roller Coasters & Amusement Parks

America's Top
Roller Coasters
& Amusement Parks

A Guide for Those
who Ride Them

and Tips for
Those who
Fear Them

Pete Trabucco

TATE PUBLISHING *& Enterprises*

Published by Tate Publishing & Enterprises, LLC
127 E. Trade Center Terrace | Mustang, Oklahoma 73064 USA
1.888.361.9473 | www.tatepublishing.com

Tate Publishing is committed to excellence in the publishing industry. The company reflects the philosophy established by the founders, based on Psalm 68:11,
"The Lord gave the word and great was the company of those who published it."

Book design copyright © 2009 by Tate Publishing, LLC. All rights reserved.
Cover design by Lance Waldrop
Interior design by Stephanie Woloszyn
All images courtesy of Joel Rogers of Coaster Gallery, http://www.coastergallery.com

Published in the United States of America

ISBN: 978-1-60696-645-7
1. Biography
2. Roller Coaster/Leisure
09.10.27

Dedication

There were many people who I would like to thank for the publication of this book. First and foremost, I would like to thank my daughter, Jennifer who by coming into my life gave me the strength to challenge my fears (both at the parks and on these pages) and conquer them. I guess it takes a kid to make you feel like one and I am forever grateful that God had selected me to be her Dad. Also, I don't think anyone can undertake something like this without the backing of their significant others. Twenty years ago, I married my wife Dorie and again hit the jackpot! She is my best friend, my mentor and has had to endure many trips to these parks and many hours of research with me in order to see this work in print. Thanks, dear, I love ya! I would also like to thank my parents, Mary and Pete, Sr. who have always been there for me and continue to support me every day. Finally, I like to thank the many people I have met over the years who like myself have a passion (and sometimes had the fear) for riding the rails. Without their feedback and advice, I would not have been able to complete this book.

"Sometimes out of darkness, one can see the light of conquest."

Pete

Table of Contents

The Search for
the Ultimate Scream Machine

On the following pages, you will learn more about the ultimate scream machines around the country that I have been lucky enough to ride on over the last several years. Many of these coasters have consistently been represented on many of the top one hundred roller coaster lists distributed throughout the nation. I can honestly tell you that I have truly enjoyed each and every one of these rides and look forward to riding these coasters again! Whether you prefer wood coasters or today's steel mega-marvels, from that coaster seat, you really get the chance to experience the world from an entirely new and very different perspective. Like flying an airplane (which is another one of my hobbies), your viewpoint of the world vastly changes and can help in altering how you perceive yourself. Also, where else can you ride something that will exhilarate you and scare the heck out of you all at the same time? But the best part is that not only can you ride and scream your head off on these roller coasters, but you can get to experience it with someone you love as well.

With thousands of new gravity-defying contraptions across the nation, and more cropping up every day, roller coasters and thrill rides truly are the driving forces behind any amusement park and in most cases are the sole basis of that amusement park's very existence. In the last several years, America has experienced a renaissance in the creation of new roller coasters, and because of this, you have seen many great advances in roller coaster technology. You can literally see this occurring in today's newest coasters in terms of their overall size, height, and production time.

You can now find many different types of roller coasters around the country that will surely amaze you. There are now flying coasters (such as *Superman, Batwing,* and *Stealth*); linear induction coasters (like *Rock n Roller Coaster* at MGM Disney World, or *Volcano* at Paramount's Kings Dominion); floorless wonders *(Medusa* and *Kraken)* and mega coasters like *Millennium Force* at Cedar Point and *Superman Ride of Steel* at Six Flags New England. There are now four-dimensional coasters (like *X* at Six Flags Magic Mountain); and just recently two new super-hydraulic mega coasters have come into the mix, with the introduction of the 420-foot marvel *Top Speed Dragster* at Cedar Point in Sandusky, Ohio, and the 455-foot behemoth *Kingda Ka* at Six Flags Great Adventure. All of these new rides seem to exhibit extended ride elements that seem to defy or at least bend the laws of physics, as we know them. In this industry, the sky is the limit and the possibilities now seem to be endless. Indeed it is a great time to be a roller coaster enthusiast.

But why do people ride these coasters in the

Superman Ride of Steel (now called Bizarro) at Six Flags New England

Pete Trabucco

first place? Why subject yourself to the terror? The anticipation and screams you witness while waiting in line for such rides? And why subject yourself to that moment of truth when those ride gates open, and you find yourself strapping in like a test pilot to the latest contraption and heading up a towering lift hill, if there is even a lift hill to head up?

I guess there is something to be said for facing your fears head on, and that is why most people do it. What was it that President Franklin D. Roosevelt once said regarding overcoming the fear element in life? He said, "There is nothing to fear but fear itself." His statement was not intended for a coaster enthusiast, yet it goes a long way in explaining why people challenge themselves on these roller coasters and other thrill rides. It seems that facing your fears head on and overcoming them really does make you feel good about yourself and the world that you live in. I guess that's the challenge of trying new and different things, and in coastering (as in most other things) in general, it's a doorway to one more new and different experience in life. It brings out the classic fight or flight impulse embedded in all of us, a behavior very evident when it comes to these mega coaster thrill rides and ultimately, our own secret fears.

People ride coasters for many different reasons. Some just love the thrill of trying something new, different, and exciting. Others see it as a way to unload their stress after a hard day's work. Still others want to be challenged and see how far they can push their own physical and emotional envelopes, or what I like to call the "pucker factor." (That factor will make you break out in a cold hard sweat and have your mouth and lips sucking for as much air as possible.) After all, where else can you scream your head off without getting arrested in today's society! I am sure if you ask ten people why they ride coasters, you will get ten different answers. Everyone has a story to tell. All of them are interesting and seem to follow a logical path as to why we "coaster." It appears that the main reason why people who come from all walks of life, called "adrenaline junkies," partake in such activity is to overcome a fear and to experience "life on the edge." The final group of coaster riders can be categorized as those who truly want to experience this thrill but, alas, can't seem to take that first step past their fear.

The intention of this book is to explore the best coasters and parks around the country—to find out what makes these rides so breathtaking and to help you thrill riders make your choices on where to sit and when is the best time to ride the rails. But it is also written to help those of you who simply fear coasters and just want to overcome your fears of these behemoths of the midway. It is actually at this point that my story begins and is the main reason why I wrote about this topic.

Roller Coasters— Closing the Loop! (My Story)

This could be classified as a strange story, but one that I feel I must share with you. It is a classic story of a simple man's journey through his own fear toward overall mental health and enlightenment—a man who, for most of his life, was afraid of roller coasters and other thrill rides. Then, at the age of forty, I was able finally to see things from a different perspective and see the drops and thrills at amusement parks for what they really are—an exciting experience that will always take your breath away and have you craving more. Let me explain!

When I was around six, my parents put me on one of those kiddy coasters at an amusement park somewhere on the east coast. My mom was frightened for me when she sat me down on this ride and gave me the strangest look. The expression on her face instinctively told me that she feared she would never, ever see me again. Well as you can guess, I was scared, afraid, and petrified, crying throughout the entire ride. As you also might have guessed, that would be the end of the story for me on roller coasters, or so I thought. I decided that these rides were not for me.

Fast forward to my teenage years. Yes, I would go to all the hot carnivals and amusement parks in the area and for the most part would have a fair time at them. However, that usually changed when someone suggested, "Let's go on that coaster," or "Wow, what a drop on that one," or "That coaster really looks like fun!"

You can guess what came next. "No thanks, that ride looks stupid!" or my other classic reply, "The line is way too long!"

That response was met with the usual retort from my friends. You guessed it. They would tease me. "Chicken! Wimp!" followed by several expletives which those who chose not to ride coasters usually heard. They would then go on the ride and have a fantastic time, and I…Well, you get the picture.

The preceding paragraph makes it look like I was afraid of everything under the sun, but if you knew me, you would know that this statement wasn't true. Being cautious by nature never stopped me from participating in varsity baseball and football during my high school and college days. Nor did it dissuade me from earning a private pilot's license and learning how to fly aerobatic maneuvers. You know, like loops! But talk to me about roller coasters or other wild rides at your local amusement park, and that six-year-old would come to the surface of my psyche. My answer was always the same: "No way, man! Not coasters. What, are you crazy?" This proclamation became my friend for many years. After all, I could cling to the notion that "in a car or an airplane I had *control* of my environment. On a roller coaster I didn't have this control, and for anyone who doesn't get what

coasters are about, that can be terrifying! Besides, all roller coasters simply weren't safe. End of story!

That same line from my parents (God, I love them) when I was first introduced to coasters, back when I was five or six, still rang loudly in my ears many years later. If I had known then about the studies showing that a person has a better chance of being struck by lightning, several times, than of having a fatal injury on a coaster, perhaps things would have been different. In hindsight, I really wish I had done that research sooner.

It was a tough time for my friends, who were real roller coaster enthusiasts. My poor wife suffered the most. She really loved all rides, especially coasters. The crazier they were, the better, and unfortunately, she usually sat on the sidelines, or worse, had to go on the latest coasters and thrill rides all by herself. I felt guilty for making her do that, so neither one of us would have the greatest of times at these amusement parks.

Fast forward to 1996. We had a beautiful, bouncing, baby girl. By 1998 I was ready for my biggest challenge! There was no way that my little girl was going to miss out on coaster fun because of my fear. So I decided to conquer one of my biggest fears, and I put together a battle plan to once and for all get rid of my childhood fear of roller coasters. The battle would begin in the state of New Jersey but wouldn't end there. I would start with medium-sized coasters (I was okay on the really small ones), and work my way up to the top woodies and steel rides all around the nation. That was the plan. I figured with this strategy, it would take around five years to overcome my fear.

But something happened along the way. I grew up! I realized that I was no longer a child but an adult who actually liked to try new experiences. Unfortunately until then, I was stuck with my childhood preconception of what roller coasters were supposed to be like and did not have the ability to move on. It took a very special roller coaster (and let's be honest, any real coaster that you first ride, accept, and enjoy can apply here) to show me that the frightened child in me was gone and the adult, who sometimes acted like a child, had successfully put the past behind him.

You can always tell a coaster fanatic by the way he or she talks about his or her first real experience on a roller coaster. Sure I had ridden the local mine trains every now and then, closed my eyes and hoped for the best, but I did not experience a real coaster until 1998. It was called *Rolling Thunder* out of Six Flags Great Adventure in New Jersey, a slow, rough, loud and rickety old coaster by today's standards, but boy, when I finally let go of my fears, what a ride I received that day! I actually don't remember much from the first ride, but the most important thing had been accomplished. *I did it* and lived to tell the tale. That was all that mattered! So I decided to try the ride again, and guess what? It actually was a lot of fun. I proceeded to spend the rest of the year on rides that I never thought I would ever even go near. I started to ride other wood coasters, and there was another great one in New Jersey called *Great White* located at Morey's Pier in Wildwood. From there, I rode such classics as the *Cyclone* in New York City, *Ghost Rider* in San Diego, *Boulder Dash* in Connecticut, and *The*

Texas Giant in Alrlington, Texas and *The Comet* at Six Flags in Lake George, New York.

It was now time to tackle the big steel coasters the nation had to offer. There were literally hundreds of steel coasters to choose from. A steel coaster ride is extremely different from a wood coaster experience, in that on a steel coaster, the rider receives a much smoother and faster ride than on wood coasters. Because steel can be bent into many different shapes, the riders can be dropped down or catapulted up many types of loops and inversions that you can't do on wood.

Steel coasters can be built as high as a thirty-story building. These are called mega coasters, and you can attain top speeds of almost one hundred miles per hour, as in *Superman the Escape* at Six Flags Magic Mountain in California does. A wood coaster's appeal is in the "out of control" feeling that you get when riding one. They are generally louder than steel coasters as they clank and plummet down the track at speeds of forty to sixty miles per hour. Even though they are not as fast as steel coasters, in many ways they are as much fun as their steel offspring. Besides, I started this adventure with them, and wood coasters will always hold a special place in my journey.

So wood was conquered, and steel was next on my list. I started my conquest of steel and picked coasters like *Batman* and a floorless coaster by the name of *Medusa* at Six Flags Great Adventure in New Jersey to start me off. Not bad, but like a hungry tiger on the prowl, and no longer weighed down by my fears, I wanted (and needed) more! So from there I went to Massachusetts and tackled *Superman Ride of Steel* at Six Flags New England, one of the best coasters and tallest in the world! What a ride! I then decided to check out the *Incredible Hulk* and *Dueling Dragons* at Universal Studios Florida, and since I happened to be in the neighborhood, *Kraken* at SeaWorld and *Rock n Roller Coaster* at Disney World seemed to be the next rides on my roller coaster adventure. Of course one of the tallest coasters in the world, *Millennium Force,* had to be included, and the list goes on…

What follows is a total of 300 new and exciting roller coasters, as well as three dozen top amusement

Pete Trabucco

parks to visit around the country. You name it and chances are I have been on it. To date, I have ridden forty of the nation's top fifty combined coasters (wood and steel) that *Amusement Park Today,* the amusement park industry's top-rated trade newspaper, lists as top coasters in the country. I also take advantage of all drop towers, water rides, and other high-energy action that you can find at these amusement parks. In the near future, I plan on visiting Europe and riding the best of the best there as well. At this point, there are no boundaries or borders when it comes to riding coasters for me.

And thanks to my efforts and without coaxing— Ok, maybe just a little coaxing my little girl, who by the way, is now six-years old, has ridden thirty-four roller coasters around the country as well. Like her dad, she has a scrap book at home of all her coaster accomplishments and has the pictures and statistics to back them up. This is truly something that we share, and I am sure we will be able to do this for many years to come. What a big difference from the way I spent my childhood, and I am glad for that.

It seems to me that the people who invented these rides had us in mind when they created them, and thanks to them and the new wave of safe but exciting thrill rides, we are now in the midst of experiencing a new renaissance in the industry.

So you say, how did this happen? How did a cautious person like me morph into a roller coaster fanatic able to tackle the tallest and fastest coasters this nation has to offer? I really couldn't tell you. But like all of you, I can safely say that screaming loudly on the ride sure seems to help. For it is a proven fact that those who scream really don't feel the drops (something about blood rushing to the head) and usually come off the ride feeling fantastic and ready to tackle the next challenge. Most importantly, I just took the chance, believed in myself, and in doing so was rewarded for my efforts. Every aspect, from the anticipation of riding the new mega-marvels to the rides themselves, not to mention the thrill of watching your child's reaction on these wonderful contraptions, is more than enough enjoyment.

This should also be a lesson to all those who fear

coasters. I tell people that your fear of coasters (or anything for that matter) can be erased forever if you are willing to make the commitment to tackle this fear head on. "Why not just try it," I say! If you enjoy it, you just might be forever hooked on them. If you don't enjoy the ride, the worse thing that could happen is that you might feel woozy and maybe a bit disoriented when you get off. Now how bad is that? We all know that the industry has an exemplary safety record and that you are thousands of times more likely to receive personal injury driving to and from an amusement park than you are while riding a roller coaster.

Anyway, in both scenarios, the chances are pretty good that you will be talking about that ride for weeks, maybe even years to come—that is, if you still have a voice left after your adventure. And that, folks, is the main point of my story! A wise person once told me, "To live and encounter for one's self is far better than sitting around watching others experience life firsthand." Take that from me! The former is far more life enriching and gratifying than the latter. Even if you never ride the new mega roller coasters, there is so much to see and do at these parks (especially at any of the Disney parks, but we will get into that another time), that your trip will be well worth the price of any admission. Take it from me, the person voted least likely to write this book. You are never too old nor too young to try something new, feel the rush, and in doing so erase your fears!

You might ask, what does my wife think of all this? Well, that's another story for another day. I can tell you that she is in fact a little shocked at my recent strange behavior and has attributed my sudden enjoyment of roller coasters to a mid-life crisis. She might be right in that respect, but I might add is also extremely happy that my outside interests lie with these new large behemoths of the midway, rather than in the latest blonde or brunette at work.

A Brief History of Coasters—
Then and Now

So where did the concept of roller coasters come from? You might say it started when mankind decided that it might be fun to roll down hills, with or without some kind of apparatus, just to see what happened. Not very comfortable but you can be pretty sure it left a lasting impression on the participant. It is uncontested that the first gravity slides were created in the fifteenth century, when someone had the brilliant idea to create a wooden ramp, freeze the water and, well, slide down the ice. They were called "ice slides" and were very popular for their time.

And so it went until the French constructed the first wood stock coasters in 1817. Two of these rides, *Les Montagnes Russes a Belleville* and *Promenades Aeriennes,* introduced wheels and axles on their cars, grooved tracks, and a primitive cable system to lift people up the slide. They didn't go very fast, but these mechanical contraptions were very popular and seemed to be popping up all the Europe.

Fast forward to America, where the father of all coaster inventors appeared. His name was La Marcus Thompson, and this inventor would forever change the way we look at coasters. Primitive and small, the La Marcus Thompson Switchback Railway opened at New York City's Coney Island beach on June 13, 1884, and officially created the craze we still enjoy today. The ride featured two parallel straight tracks with raised platforms at either end. The rider got on at the top and, after the ride ended, got off at the bottom. Not very fast (top speed of about six miles per hour), but people would wait in lines as long as three hours to ride this innovation. Thompson created many switchback

Leap-The-Dips...The worlds oldest roller coaster

(or scenic) railways over the years, but the six hundred-foot long wonder at Coney Island was the catalyst which triggered the craze. In 1904, the Philadelphia Toboggan Company was formed, and in 1915, John Miller took over the reins and created new innovations such as anti-rollback and under-wheel devices to make the coasters much safer.

The "Golden Age" of coasters had begun. And thanks to Miller and other influential coaster designers like Fred Church, Frank Prior, Harry Baker and Arthur Looff (names familiar to any roller coaster enthusiast) during the first golden age, there were over 1500 coasters rolling around the country.

Coasters were extremely popular until the great depression hit in 1929, when most of the country's great amusement parks either closed or changed names. Usually the parks were destroyed "accidentally" by fire or by the hand of a real estate developer. It is amazing to me that even today some of these coasters still exist, but they do, hanging on to the innovations that keep them in a special place in everyone's heart.

Walt Disney took the coaster concept to the

next level when in 1955 he created Disneyland in Anaheim, California. Along with Arrow Development Company, he created the first tubular steel coaster with polyurethane-wheeled, rolling stock cars, and he called it the *Matterhorn Bobsleds*. Well, since that innovation, the rest you might say is history. Thanks to the visionaries in coaster technology, it is not uncommon to see coasters in this millennium that almost seem to touch the clouds at over 400 feet tall, while sending their passengers traveling around the track at speeds of over 125 miles per hour. Coasters are indeed the craze of the new millennium, and one that I hope you will be able to share with your loved ones.

Corkscrew at Cedar Point

Is This Ride Safe?

One of the biggest fears most people have regarding roller coasters (or any thrill ride) is that they feel that these scream machines are unsafe. They hear the creaking of an old wood coaster or see the sway in the steel of a new fangled impulse ride and—they are done! The truth of the matter is that you will not find an industry more safety conscious than the amusement park industry. After all, this industry lives and breathes on its success or failure. Any major accident and bang, you're out of business!

The truth of the matter is that going to an amusement park is one of the safest forms of recreation you can find. As a pilot, I can say that flying airplanes is pretty safe. Some may disagree with me, but if you look at the statistics, flying an airplane is much safer than operating a car. So the question arises, is flying safer than riding a roller coaster or any other thrill ride you would find at an amusement park? The answer is no! How about riding a motorcycle or a bike? Are riding these machines safer than coasters? According to the International Association of Amusement Park Attractions, the answer is again no. According to their study, you are more likely to be injured when you play sports, ride a horse, drive a car, or yes even ride a bike than when you coaster. Statistics show that the occurrence of death on an amusement park ride is approximately 1 in 250 million. You have a better chance of being struck by lightning several times.

These statistics are supported by the National Consumer Products Safety Commission, which says that more than 120 million people visit amusement parks yearly. Their findings indicate that only 7,000 of this 120 million end up at an emergency room. These incidents include falls at the local park, restaurant mishaps, and other non-ride incidents. Even when you add these injuries, a mere 0.000259 percent of all amusement park goers will actually get hurt at an amusement park. I will take those percentages every time!

Out of those injuries that do occur at amusement parks, the above reports also state that a great portion of ride injuries happened through no fault of the ride or its manufacturer. It occurred because someone—the ride operator or the rider himself—disregarded the safety rules and took unnecessary chances in order to increase the thrill factor on the ride. We hear stories all the time of people undoing their restraints while a ride is in progress or trying to stand up at the most inopportune moments. Or the kid who is too small for the restraints but somehow gets on the ride anyway. And finally let's add to the statistics the hundreds of passengers who have had chronic back or neck injuries, but due to their excitement have forgotten about their medical condition prior to riding.

In order to be fair, I will mention that these reports also concluded that in some very rare cases, the ride was poorly maintained and that better maintenance of the attraction could have prevented injury, but this was classified as a rare event. The truth is that unlike the car you drive every day, a roller coaster, as well as all other rides at an amusement park, is inspected on a daily basis. You can rest assured that at every amusement park, experienced mechanics and hi-tech computer personnel watch carefully to ensure that all of the equipment is running at top mechanical and electrical condition. This job needs to be accomplished every day and there can be no cutting corners! Also, in addition to the daily inspections in the off-season (if you live in the east), the entire ride gets a complete overhaul by licensed mechanics, computer specialists, electricians and carpenters who work at the park full time. You might have noticed in the southern parks of the United States where the weather is better (so the park doesn't close down) that a particular ride might be closed for weeks at a time. This is what they are doing, making sure the ride passes all ride safety criteria, so that it is safe for you and thousands of others to ride.

So the next time you climb that lift hill or get shot like a cannon out of a train station, spin uncontrollably or drop like a rock, please take comfort in the fact that many people are working hard every day to make sure your ride experience is a safe and enjoyable one.

High Roller at the Stratosphere Tower in Las Vegas

Fighting the Fear of Coasters:
Family Coasters Are the Ticket

So how does one get over their fear of roller coasters and thrill rides? The question is easy but sometimes the answer can be quite difficult. Every individual is different but people tend to fall into two categories when it comes to answering this question. There are those like my wife who tackle their fear by hitting it head on…They take the fear on and will challenge the biggest and baddest coasters out there. The idea behind this is that once you have conquered the biggest and the best there is the offer, you have accomplished your task in one quick swoop. I envy those individuals in that they can have the nerve to accomplish this as quickly as possible. The other group takes a 180-degree or opposite approach to this quandary. I can relate to these individuals in that, like them, I have had to tackle this challenge in stages. I can remember going to the amusement parks when I was younger. I heard the comments from my peers and the way they seem to want to pressure me or just plain embarrass me so I would relent in riding roller coasters. I don't think it was fully intentional but by using the peer pressure method, they were actually creating a reverse effect on me, which made it even more difficult for me to ride those crazy contraptions with them.

For those in the second category, I am here to tell you that this approach always fails in the end. Sure, the person in question might ride with you but, never and I mean never will you see them subject themselves to this kind of peer pressure again. I actually hated to go with them to these parks and came up with excuses all the time not to go. I knew what was going to happen and let's just say the feeling of being put on the spot like that was not very appealing.

The best approach to helping someone overcome his or her fear of roller coasters or anything else for that matter is to take it slow. Don't push them into doing something they don't want to do and in the end let them make it their choice to say yes or no to the experience. They have to want to do this and all the teasing, prodding and name calling won't help them overcome this fear. I can speak for myself that the childhood fear I had was deep and it would take the birth of my daughter to tackle this childhood nightmare. However, like many people, I needed to do this in stages and not all at once. I would not go hiking the Grand Canyon or climbing the tallest mountain that I could find as my first venture. Nor would I do this when riding roller coasters. For many others as well as myself, it makes sense to start small and build up your confidence before looking to increase the thrill level Also, I like to check the ride out and watch others before I go. Looking at the track, anticipating the drops, turns and loops makes it easer when you are unfamiliar with the ride. It's sort of like the experience I had when I was going for my FAA check ride as a pilot. I would imagine the maneuvers and go over it in my head several times until I got it right. Well on these thrill rides you can get yourself mentally (as well as physically) prepared for what lies ahead by watching the track, the riders and the coaster itself. I found that the best way to go about this was to start with these family coasters that you can easily find at most amusement parks around the country.

A family roller coaster is one that is made for the whole family to enjoy and they generally are not too wild or intense in nature. The bigger and more extreme coasters will get your pucker factor up and your adrenalin pumping while subjecting you to high g-forces that fighter pilots usually experience. As a pilot, I can tell you it takes a little time and practice to get accustomed to this level of intensity. It is not advisable to start out with this type of ride, especially for those individuals who like to have control in their lives. If they start with these family coasters, however, they can experience the fun of a roller coaster in an enjoyable and non-threatening way. Once you begin to see roller coasters as fun, even the extreme rides look a little more interesting. One other thing! I mentioned breathing (and screaming) on the ride. This is extremely important.

You'd be surprised how many people hold their breath when going down the most exciting elements of a ride. Do not do this! Not only should you breathe during the ride but especially during the big drops, wild turns and crazy elements, it would be advisable to scream your lungs out. Medically the effect of this screaming is to keep the blood flow up in your upper body and head, thus decreasing your chances of blacking out or experiencing tunnel vision on a wild ride. Also, on steep drops the negative-g effect on a person can be minimized by simply yelling or screaming at that point in the ride. What this means is that you won't feel that discomfort in your stomach region (as much) when experiencing this aspect of the ride. The same can be said when

being whipped around turns and loops in a high positive-g environment. Relax; you're on a ride, so it is really okay to yell. You will notice everyone else doing it, and if it works for them, it will also work for you.

Lastly, for those people who feel that coasters are unsafe, be assured that coasters are much safer than just about any other activity. Your chances of receiving bodily injury are hundreds of times greater when you get into your car and drive to the park. In fact, statistics show that you have a better chance of being struck by lightning than receiving a major injury on a roller coaster, so relax and enjoy the ride. Remember, riding a coaster gives the illusion of being unsafe, but the fact is that the roller coaster industry is one of the most safety-conscious industries out there. NASA should take as many precautions as they do.

So now that you are ready to start your adventure, how do you go about doing it? Well, earlier I said that a good way to start is to plan your coaster acclimation to start with some family coasters. Here are some examples of these roller coasters, which can be found around the country.

- *Flying Unicorn* at Islands of Adventure, Universal Orlando, Florida. A standard Vekoma junior "roller skater" coaster, this is a nice ride to try out before you try the big-name coasters at this park like *The Hulk* and *Dueling Dragons*. At 2000 feet long and reaching speeds of nearly 30 miles per hour, this one is great for the kids as well as their parents. The wooded area is in the Jurassic Park section of the park, and the biggest drop on this coaster is only around thirty feet.

- *Blackbeard's Lost Treasure Train* (At Six Flags Great Adventure, Jackson, NJ) made by Zierer (Tivoli) Company is a junior roller coaster, and if you're at Six Flags Great Adventure in New Jersey this is one that the whole family can enjoy. It stands twenty-six feet high with a twenty-five-foot first drop and several twisting turns on what can only be described as one of the longest trains ever created. This single train has a total of twenty cars (sitting two abreast) for a total of forty riders. The train is so long that the whipping action in the back end of the ride is comparable to an intermediate coaster of double its size, and often the last several rows are actually closed off to riders. The ride twists around the 1164-foot track at speeds approaching twenty-five miles per hour. In the United States there are ten similar coasters operating in the United States. You can ride the same type of coaster under the name of *Poison Ivy's Tangled Train* at Six Flags New England, *Roadrunner Express* at Six Flags and World of Adventure, and *Timber Twister* at Bonfante Gardens in Oregon. Larger custom versions of this Tivoli classic can also be found at Knott's Berry Farm in California under the name *Jaguar* and in the indoor Mall of America at Camp Snoopy in Minnesota under the name of the *Pepsi Ripsaw*.

- *Big Thunder Mountain Railroad* at Disneyland,

Big Thunder Mountain Railroad at the Magic Kingdom at Walt Disney World, Lake Buena Vista, Florida

Anaheim, CA, and the Magic Kingdom at Walt Disney World, Lake Buena Vista, Florida was one of the first mine trains I rode at Disney and is a great one for beginners, Its not very fast (about 30MPH) and for those who hate drops... good news! This one doesn't have any. There are two different versions of this ride. One in Florida and the other in California. Both are fast but personally, I like the one in California. Disney takes rides that already exist and always makes them better. Such is true with both rides and they are definitely rides you will enjoy with the kids. On most e-ticket type rides at Disney, it is best if you easy-pass this one instead of waiting the hour or so just remember easy pass runs tickets sometimes run out so don't wait till the end of the day top get them.

- *Star Jet* at Casino Pier in Seaside Heights, New Jersey is a great little coaster. If you are looking for some fun overlooking the Atlantic Ocean, you will enjoy this family coaster built by the

Star Jet at Casino Pier in Seaside Heights, New Jersey

Miler Coasters of Portland, Oregon. This purple steel-track coaster replaced none other than the classic Schwarzkopf *Jet Star* coaster. I will admit that when they took the *Jet Star* down, I was a little disappointed. However, the new *Star Jet* provides a completely new experience, with more airtime than its predecessor had. Standing at fifty-two feet high and starting you off with a swooping right-hand turn and drop to the right, this coaster is great for beginners as well as experienced coaster enthusiasts. As you climb the lift hill, you are literally over the ocean, and as you make that first turn toward the first drop, you can look straight down and see the waves (and sometimes fish) crashing below you. Built in 2002, this coaster is a pleasant surprise and a welcome addition to the *Wild Mouse* coaster (also from Miler) that shares this pier. The three-car (two per car) setup also ensures that there isn't a bad seat in the house.

- *Vapor Trail* at Sesame Place in Pennsylvania is a good family coaster to ride. This specially crafted enhanced Vekoma roller skater stands at fifty feet tall and takes riders down a 1300-foot track at almost thirty miles per hour. This is a junior coaster but can be ridden and enjoyed by adults as well. I would recommend this coaster for any beginner or intermediate coaster enthusiast who also enjoys wet and wild water parks. Pleasing their guests since 1998, *Vapor* has enhanced park patrons' experience by bringing an added dimension to what was primarily a water park. Since the track is so small, only one train can be used, accommodating only twenty people at a time. Even so, lines are never too long at this attraction. From the lift hill, you can scan the park area and see blue water from several adjacent water attractions in every direction, as you get ready for your ride. But do not blink, you just might miss it. *Vapor Trail* is a fun ride for everyone!

Matterhorn Bobsleds at Disneyland, Anaheim, California

Pete Trabucco

- *Matterhorn Bobsleds* at Disneyland, Anaheim, California. This is the first steel track ever to be created. Arrow development did the honors back in 1959. The ride is not big (about 80 feet height) it is not fast (about 19 MPH) but you and your family will love it. Most of the ride is situated in the mountain and is in the dark. Disney would have similar success with *Space Mountain* on these types of dark rides. Even though it is quite slow as compared to other coasters, the design of this ride is the beauty is in its design and feeling of illusion. Like the later version, *Space Mountain coaster*, two tracks were created for this ride. A good idea since I can't imagine how long this ride would be if they only had the one. They are slightly different from each other because they weave in and out of the scaled-down version of an actual mountain range (that Walt himself visited) in Switzerland. Kids as well as adults just love the abominable snowman (as opposed to the one at Expedition Everest in Orlando Florida) and the ice caves that can be seen inside this manmade mountain ride. Also, inside the mountain you will find red-eyed bats that frequent these caves. It's Disney magic at its best!

- *Woody Woodpecker's Nuthouse Coaster* at Universal Studios Florida. It's a cute ride and one that doesn't really have long lines. It might be small and cramped with a long queue, but I assure you that it is well worth the wait. The steepest drop on this Vekoma roller skater coaster is just around twenty feet, and the top speed will only reach twenty-two mph. However, as stated earlier, higher and faster are not always better.

- *Gadget's Go Coaster* at Disneyland is simply a fun kiddy coaster. Situated in the ToonTown section of the park, this junior Vekoma roller skater is colorful and pretty quick for its size. The roller skater coaster is one of Vekoma's most successful mass-produced creations, with over fifty currently running worldwide. *Gadgets*

Gadget's Go Coaster at Disneyland

Pete Trabucco

Goofy's Barnstormer at the Magic Kingdom in Walt Disney World adds another element to it, because as you go through one of the helixes, some passengers on board the train will get wet. This is accomplished by certain water spouts that shoot streams of water out from a strategic location around the ride. The *Gadget* coaster is twenty-eight feet high and takes kids and nervous parents alike through a maze of small tight turns and twists, but don't worry. The coaster rarely reaches the double digits on the miles per hour meter. Other roller skater coasters are *Goofy's Barnstormer* at Magic Kingdom in Walt Disney World Florida, and the nearby *Woody Woodpecker's Nuthouse* at Universal Studios Florida.

• *Goofy's Barnstormer* at the Magic Kingdom in Walt Disney World is a fast little junior coaster created by Vekoma Corporation. This standard roller skater coaster stands twenty-eight feet tall, uses two trains, and themes the experience as would a runaway plane. During its 790-foot run around the track, the colorful coaster goes through a barn, around tight turns, and down one twenty-foot first drop. A great coaster for the young and the young-at-heart, this coaster reaches a top speed of twenty-two miles per hour. You can find Goofy and his bi-plane in the ToonTown section of the park.

Now these are just a few examples of the smaller coasters you will find out there. The idea is to work up to bigger and better roller coasters and the next set are just that. They are bigger faster and wilder. The first one on the list is one of my favorites…

• *Space Mountain* at Disneyland, Anaheim, California, and a second one can be found at the Magic Kingdom at Walt Disney World, Lake Buena Vista, Florida. Anyone who has ridden these rides will tell you that when you fly down the tracks on this ride, it's like riding through space while moving at 30 miles per hour. You are in the dark except for the stars, moons and comets that fly past you during the ride. The rides are different from each other in that the Magic Kingdom version emphasizes twists and sharp turns with slight drops, while the Disneyland version (along with a space-y soundtrack) emphasizes sheer speed and smoothness throughout the ride. Both *Space Mountains* are great rides. They are worth the wait, which can average forty-five minutes unless you use the easy pass program. Through Disney's magic and ability to create illusion, both rides feel much faster than the reported top speed of just twenty-nine mph. The innovative queue set up also makes these two destination coasters a good next step on your roller coaster adventure. Whichever one you prefer, there is no doubt that these two (actually, there are four tracks, two for each ride) are classics and ones that you will surely enjoy.

• *Runaway Mountain* at Six Flags over Texas, Arlington, Texas. Created in 1996 by Premier, this ride is similar to *Space Mountain* without the

Space Mountain at Disneyland, Anaheim, California

themes or illusory atmosphere—it's pitch dark inside—and I am told is a is a slightly modified *Windstorm* production coaster. It will drop its guests thirty feet and will reach top speeds of up to forty mph during its 1500-foot long track. It's a heart-pounding, mysterious adventure, especially for those who don't like the dark, and is a hidden treasure at this park. Twist and turn through this giant mountain while hidden somewhere in these grounds, it has been said, awaits a bountiful treasure! With its near fifty degree drops, ninety-two degree banked angles, and two high-speed horizontal spirals, it's a good coaster to ride and will set you up for the next level of coasters on your list.

- *Skull Mountain* at Six Flags Great Adventure in Jackson, New Jersey is a good coaster for those who have graduated from the junior coaster league and want to try something a little more exciting. Built by Interman and Giovanola in 1986, this indoor coaster has just about everyone guessing where you will go next. Starting off in a themed cave-like station, riders get to negotiate through a darkened cave-like building in order to get to their destination. The ride is very dark (unlike *Space Mountain*) which adds to the illusion of speed and danger. When they say *Skull Mountain*, they aren't kidding. The rocky exterior on the front of the building includes a giant skull-like image and dual waterfalls protruding from the eyes. The actual ride is not very long, and its top speed never goes past forty miles per hour. Also, at forty-one feet high, you don't really feel that first forty-seven foot drop, but you will enjoy the tight turns and total darkness, which definitely confuses your senses during the 1300-plus foot trek. Since only one train runs at a time, lines can get quite long, so you might want to allow yourself some time for this one. I enjoy the front seat for this ride because you can just make out the track and see how close you really come to the exterior of the ride itself. It is also a good warm-up for the e-ticket rides (*Nitro*, *Superman*, and *Medusa*) located at this park.

- *The Jack Rabbit Coaster* at Clementon Park, New Jersey was built in 1917 and is the second-oldest coaster in the country. (The only coaster in America that is older is *Leap for Dips* which was created in 1902.) Standing at fifty feet high and overlooking most of the park, this ride shoots you down several hills at speeds that reach forty miles per hour. Created by the legend himself, John Miller, this 1700-foot long figure eight design originally ran trains that were not operated with up-stops, which limited the experience quite a bit. New trains were added in 1999 and the ride is much better (wilder) than it was. It is truly a family coaster and one that just about everyone would love. Since trees, foliage and other rides hide most of this coaster, those who want to see it in action before they ride should go on the little park train below. The park train will give you the "lay of the land" and a great view of the

The Jack Rabbit Coaster

ride. But beware, there are elephants, bears, and other wild animals roaming around this area as well. You will know they are not real by the paint that seems to be peeling off most of them as you ride by. Still, the kids will enjoy it! The *Jack Rabbit* is a fast and enjoyable little woodie, and one that I highly recommend. You rather get the feeling that if this ride could talk, the stories it might be able to tell you…

• *The Comet* at Hershey Park, Hershey, Pennsylvania. Classified by ACE as a classic wood coaster, the Comet dates back to 1946 and is one of the biggest coasters ever created at that time. Designed by Herbert Schmeck, and built by the Philadelphia Toboggan Company, this coaster has a modified double out and back design. I especially like the first drop suspended over the water. This ride has an eighty-foot drop and reaches a top speed of almost fifty mph. This particular drop sends riders into a hairpin turn before it drops you again on your way toward a very nice but sometimes rough coaster

experience. It creaks, cracks, and looks rickety, but in my mind, it is a gem of a coaster and one that all coaster aficionados should experience.

• *The Dragon Coaster* at Playland Park in Rye, New York was built in 1929, just after the park's debut. It was built by Fred Church and is one of the last remaining examples of his work in America. This is a very interesting ride with a unique, V-shaped layout. Standing at seventy-five feet tall with a sixty-foot drop, the *Dragon* flies riders down the 3400-foot long track at speeds reaching forty-five miles per hour. You might notice that this ride seems a little longer than it actually is. This feeling is achieved by the coaster being multi-layered, so that just when you expect the ride to end, you have another section of track to cover. It's these little surprises, which make this coaster nothing less than a classic. The *Dragon* has been featured in many movies, and one of its more memorable moments occurs when riders get to go through the dragon's mouth and can be seen exiting out its tail section. A classic coaster and one that can help set you up toward the next level of thrill rides. Note: Playland Park is a pay-as-you-go park, so you can ride this one many times without notice of any long lines.

- *Thunderbolt* at Six Flags New England, built in 1941 (just one year after the flyer *Comet* at Whalon Park), has a surprising element that very few coasters have, a double dip/drop series. This means that as you drop you stop, level off, and then drop again. It is a great ride experience for those who have never tried this type of element before and makes this coaster a classic. It is also a coaster with very few surprises and seems to deliver a consistent ride every time. For new coaster fanatics and families alike, this is one you should ride. Take advantage of *Thunderbolt* and ride this vintage family woodie at night. It's a little spooky, but in the end you will be happy you did.

Finally you are ready for this coaster…

- *The Dark Knight Coaster* is located at Six Flags Great Adventure in Jackson, New Jersey. More than just a mouse ride, *The Dark Knight* coaster features the most world-beloved DC Comics characters (The Batman Crew) in an adventure that utilizes storytelling, physical movement, video, sound and special effects to bring guests a one-of-a-kind dark ride thrill. As you enter the enclosed buidling riders will believe they are part of the movie and plot line and will witness first hand the City of Gotham under attack by the Joker and his henchmen. Riders board a special car and fly through several elements that include drops in the dark and neck flinching 180-degree turns. It is said that *The Dark Knight* coaster offers guests a one-of-a-kind ride experience that combines the action and excitement of The Dark Knight movie with the thrill of a roller coaster. The $7.5 million coaster is located in the Movie Town section at Six Flags Great

Batman: The Knight Flight at Six Flags over New England

Truly a ride to experience during the completion phase of your roller coaster training.

Adventure adjacent to *Batman: the Ride*. Guests can receive up-to-the-minute park news and purchase a season pass online at www.sixflags. com.

Congratulations, you're doing great! I bet you are starting to have fun right now...That's what these rides can offer you. A chance to challenge yourself on even bigger roller coasters. When you have reached this level, you might try riding coasters like the crazy mouse spinning rides. These coasters spin you around as they traverse the circuit. When you have graduated from that level, you will then be ready for the bigger wood coasters (eighty feet or higher).

After that you can experience single or double loop and corkscrew coasters that are in the park. There are literally hundreds of these types of coasters in the country, and I am sure there is one near you. When you talk about looping and corkscrew coasters, you have reached the dividing line between those people who like coasters and those who really crave them. The loop (or inversion) can be compared to the coming-out party for the true roller coaster enthusiast. You're not really a full member of the club until you have experienced one, and here is where many, many people simply "stop the ride!" They think it is too intense or are afraid of the experience.

What I usually tell people (at my many speaking engagements, radio and television interviews) is to think of a loop as a reverse somersault in your own living room. All you have to do is go home and if in decent shape, lie down and roll yourself over backward. This will give you a similar sensation to what it actually feels like on a looping element of a roller coaster. Usually those who try a coaster inversion get over their fear very quickly, and afterwards, they usually wonder what all the fuss was about. They usually tell me that they are now ready for even more loops and inversions in the future. Just like in real life, they simply meet and conquer the challenge and move on. Riding a looping coaster is a big step, and for most people when this has been accomplished, the pathway is clear for mass-produced coasters such as boomerangs and shuttle-loop coasters.

If you are like me, you will now start to enjoy new rides and experiences. You will love multi-element inverted loops (five or more inversions) and spin rides like B&M's Batman the Ride and the many Vekoma (SLC) Mind Eraser coasters found throughout the United States. From there it's just a short putt to the best coasters built today, coasters that have wacky features (flying, compressed air launch, stand-up, floorless, and impulse coasters), and eventually you will ride the ultimate e-ticket 200-, 300-, and now 400-foot hyper coasters in these amusement parks. It is a great feeling to overcome your fear and the satisfaction you get from overcoming another challenge in your life will have successfully ended.

This completion phase creates a whole new set of challenges. Now that you love to ride, the question is, where do you go to get your next rush? Usually coaster enthusiasts travel together in clubs, like American Coaster Enthusiasts (ACE), and travel around the country looking for bigger and more exciting coasters to tackle and experience. With 7,500 members nationwide, it is safe to say that at this point you have arrived and are most likely the ACE organization's 7501st member! Good for you!

Types of Roller Coasters

There are many different types of roller coasters that have been created for our enjoyment all over the world. These coasters can be put into two distinct categories—coasters made of wood, and those made of steel. Wood coasters have been manufactured to fit into basically four different subcategories: out and back style marvels; twisters; racers; and all-terrain, or mountain coasters. Each type of coaster brings a different fear factor to the rider.

Steel coasters come in all shapes and sizes too, but again, most are manufactured to fit into a specific subcategory: wild mouse rides; mine train; loop or corkscrew; and stand-up coasters. Also there are inverted, suspended, floorless, flying, and of course the new linear induction motor roller coasters as well.

Finally, we have the biggest and baddest coasters every created, the mega (and even taller giga) coasters that seem to break just about every record and seem to lack any limits at all. They push the thrill level to a new level, and some of these coasters can reach and exceed heights of three hundred feet. At the time of this reading, several coasters stand even higher than that, having been erected to stand over 450 feet. So now that you are aware of the basic types of roller coasters out there, let's get into specifics so that you may be able to make an intelligent decision as to if or when a particular coaster would be right for you and your family.

The Mighty Wood Roller Coaster

Out and Back Coasters:

Out and back coasters are just that. They are coasters that fly down a track, have a turnaround section, and fly back toward the start, covering a lot of ground in as little time as they can. They are pretty much straightforward or L-shaped in their design and have many small hills, dips and summits that make the ride very enjoyable. On out and back coasters (as on many other types of coaster) the main element that people are looking for is airtime. That is the time when your backside is flung off your seat and into the air. This gives the feeling of negative gravitation forces and can wake your senses up in a hurry. For those unfamiliar with the feeling of negative-g's, it is sort of like taking a small hill or pump too fast in your car and getting the feeling that you are about to the hit the roof of your vehicle. Not fun in your car, but on a coaster, well it can be, for the coaster enthusiast. Some examples of out and back design coasters are *Shivering Timbers* at Michigan Adventure, *Ghostrider* (combination out and back/twister) at Knott's Berry Farm California, and the *Phoenix* at Knoebels Amusement Resort in Pennsylvania.

Twister Coasters:

Twister coasters are very different from the out and back design, in that they usually are more compact, and seem to go in and out of their own structure many times. They literally crisscross up and down into their frame to make for many curving drops, whirlpool turns, and head-bumping effects along the course. The best of these coasters are almost impossible to figure out. You will need to ride those several times in order to get a good course layout, so if you don't like surprises, you might just want to watch others ride before you come on board. Some of the most famous twisters around and still in operation today are *The Cyclone* in Coney Island, New York; *Roar* at Six Flags America, Maryland; and *The Texas Giant* at Six Flags Over Texas.

Racer Coasters:

Racer coasters add the element of competition, in that there are dual tracks and trains that go up the lift hill and course together in a mirror image of itself. Coasters of this design can be any combination of out and back/ twister designs and can be set up in a figure eight design. On this ride you see many riders trying to get as streamlined as possible in order to be more aerodynamic, in an effort to go faster and have their side of the track win the race. Some of the best

racing coasters in the country are *Lightning Racer* at Hershey Park, Pennsylvania; *Gwazi* at Busch Gardens, Florida; and *Colossus* at Six Flags Magic Mountain, California.

All-Terrain/Mountain Coasters:

Yes, terrain coasters have lift hills like most roller coasters, but as those of you who have been to many parks can concur, these parks can have uneven terrain. Hills and valleys seem to split many parks up, and as a result, at the end of the day your feet can be living proof of this statement. All-terrain coasters adhere to the contours of the landscape. They exploit ravines and mountains by using them as part of the ride structure. The great thing (or the worst thing for some riders) is that usually on these types of coasters, you can never see the course track layout and never know what is really coming next. Foliage is everywhere, and the track is obscured by the mountains, trees, and high grass. You rarely know where you are in relation to the end of the ride, unless you've ridden it a few times. That can be a problem for those coaster enthusiasts who like to know where they are and where they are going at all times. If you want to feel like going through the woods at full gallop, this type of coaster is for you. Some of the best examples of this type of coaster are the *Beast* at Paramount's Kings Island, Ohio; the *Raven* at Holiday World in Santa Claus, Indiana; and *Boulder Dash* at Lake Compounce, Connecticut.

Steel Marvels

Wild Mouse/Crazy Mouse Rides:

These are commonly referred to as family coasters in that these are great for beginners and those who want to have fun without much intensity. Yes, it may feel like you are going to go off the end of the track and plummet fifty to seventy feet onto the ground below, but for the most part these rides are less intense than the e-ticket ones at the park. They follow a track that has a series of U-turns that gradually become intense as the ride progresses. The crazy mouse versions add another element to the experience by making the car continually spin as it treks down the track. An example of a really good wild mouse is found at Hershey Park's *Wild Mouse* ride in Pennsylvania. One of the best crazy mouse rides, *Prime Evil Whirl,* can be located at Walt Disney World's Animal Kingdom.

Wild Mine Trains:

These rides give you the feeling that you are careening through a mine shaft at breakneck speeds on a runaway train. These were the first steel-production coasters and still have a place at almost every big amusement park. Again, these rides can be enjoyed by most people who are afraid of doing loops or inversions of any kind. They are generally themed for the family and give the feeling of being inside a mine in the Old West. However, that being said, some of these mine trains can now reach speeds of sixty miles per hour and have a height of over 125 feet. You can find one that big at Cedar Point, at Sandusky, Ohio named *Gemini.*

The Wild Mouse at Casino Pier in New Jersey

Pete Trabucco

Looping Coasters:

Looping coasters (although tried in the early 1900's) were not very successful until a coaster by the name of *Revolution* (Six Flags Magic Mountain California) came along in 1976. Yes, it is true that a year before, another coaster (Knott's Berry Farm's *Corkscrew*), was created to have a place in the history books as the world's first inversion coaster. But the story belongs to *Revolution,* which you can still ride today.

> NOTE: When you talk about looping and corkscrew coasters, you have reached the dividing line between those people who like coasters and those who really crave them. The loop (or inversion) can be compared to as the coming out party for the true roller coaster enthusiast. You're not really a full member of the club until you have experienced this and here is where many people simply "stop the ride!" They think it is too intense or are afraid of the experience. What I usually tell people at my many speaking engagements or when on the radio or television

shows is think of this as a reverse somersault in your house. All one has to do is go home and if in decent shape, roll oneself over backward while lying on their living room rug. Doing this will give you a similar effect as what you feel like on a smaller looping coaster. Usually those who try this get over their fear very quickly and go on to try a loop-style coaster. They usually tell me afterward that the greatest fear was in their head and that they would like to try even more inversions on coasters in the future. Just like in real life, they simply conquer their fears and move on.

Suspended Coasters:

These were the first roller coasters that had the rider hanging below the track. Unlike inverted coasters, these coasters swung from side to side, using centrifugal force, but were unable to make the rider loop or roll. These coasters, created by Arrow Development, were actually created to spin and loop, but unfortunately the actual design had many problems. If the heavy train were not traveling fast enough, there wouldn't be enough momentum to have its cars loop all the way around the track, and unfortunately the cars would simply fall to the side with tremendous force, causing injury to the rider. After many years trying to figure out the problem, the conclusion was that it would be too costly to change the design, so instead these suspended coasters make riders swing from side to side as they negotiate turns around the track. Although not as intense as inverted coasters, they are still a lot of fun to ride. The best of these suspended coasters can still be found at Busch Gardens Williamsburg named *Big Bad Wolf*, and at Six Flags Magic Mountain named *Ninja*.

Inverted Coasters:

This type of coaster is suspended from the rails above, but unlike a suspended coaster, does not swing freely. Riders are horse-collared in their seats and their feet dangle. There is literally nothing beneath your feet but the ground below. On these coasters you can do loops, corkscrews and other inversions while being strapped into you chair. It is surely a different feeling than being seated in your typical roller coaster car and can be a lot more fun. These coasters are generally smooth, and the rider takes some heavy positive-g's during the ride. If you get to this level in your coastering, baby, you have arrived and can handle just about anything that comes next. One of the most well-known rides in this category is *Batman the Ride*, with production models all over North America. The tallest inverted coaster to date is *Alpengeist*, a two hundred-foot monster located at Busch Gardens in Williamsburg, Virginia.

Stand-Up Coasters:

These are steel coasters with specially built harnesses designed to allow the passenger to ride straight up in a standing position. The company Togo of Japan first brought the concept of the stand-up coaster to America in 1984. Riding a stand-up coaster gives you a very different sensation, and most of them are kind of hard on the knees and feet, though they are still worth riding. All stand-up coasters in the United States have at least one inversion. Some have as many as five. One of the best stand-up coasters can be found at Six Flags Magic Mountain California under the name *Riddler's Revenge.* Currently there are less than a dozen of these types of rides operating in the United States.

Linear Induction Motor Roller Coasters (LIM):

Before linear induction coasters, the coaster world had to be satisfied with going up a lift hill and having gravity drop you back to earth. Sure, there were a few innovations that shot a train out of the station, but nothing that could take its passengers from zero to one hundred mph as quickly, as well as shooting them straight up and down efficiently. That was finally achieved through the use of a new propulsion system.

This type of propulsion system is accomplished by using a new concept in motor technology: the Linear Induction Motor (LIM) system. It is really a very innovative concept that propels a coaster forward on waves of electromagnetic energy. The coaster is blasted to remarkable velocity, much like being shot out of a cannon by dozens of linear induction motors strategically placed under the track This is what makes the LIM coaster different from your typical gravity (lift hill) coaster. It literally *launches* the train and its passengers down the track. This is accomplished by alternating current, which creates an electromagnetic field, generating linear motion. This form of technology was created by Premier Rides in 1996 with their first coaster, called the *Outer Limits: Flight of Fear.* You can still ride this enclosed spaghetti-track ride at Paramount's King's Dominion and King's Island if you want to. In 2005, there are literally dozens of these rides all around the nation. Some of the best can be found under the name *Mr. Freeze* at both Six Flags Over Texas and Missouri. Disney even has one located at MGM Studios in Orlando, Florida (*Rock n Roller Coaster*), and one of the very best dual track LIM coasters can be found at Six Flags New Jersey under the name *Batman and Robin: The Chiller.*

Floorless Coasters:

In 1999 B&M came up with a new concept in the roller coaster industry. Why not get the experience of an inverted coaster, but instead of having the tracks above you, rework it so the tracks are below you, and your feet are dangling just inches above these tracks. Now that can be interesting! Well, that is exactly what B&M accomplished in creating this ride. It is literally like being strapped to your favorite easy chair and flying down a series of twists, turns, and inversions at speeds in excess of sixty miles per hour. This type of ride is for those coaster enthusiasts who like to take their coaster experiences up to the next level and is not recommended for the faint of heart. The introduction of the floorless wonder called *Medusa* (now called Bizarro) at Six Flags Great Adventure in Jackson, New Jersey is just one of the many innovations that have come along in the thrill ride industry. Right now B&M have a lock on these coasters and have built several throughout the nation. You can find another floorless beauty at Six Flags Ohio under the name of *Batman Knight Flight.*

Flying Coasters:

This coaster, among all its other virtues, offers the rider a sense of flight that can be described as really intoxicating. It is accomplished using an ingenious track layout and a unique coaster car design to replicate the sensation of flight. It is literally a roller coaster where its passengers ride below and parallel to the tracks. With special harnesses made for the occupant, there is literally nothing but air separating you and the ground below. It is safe to say that no other coaster gives you the same sensation of riding below the tracks and hanging upside down. The inversions on most coasters briefly turn riders upside down, but on most flying coasters you usually maintain a down position for a large portion of the ride. At first, the urge is to hang on for dear life, but in order to truly experience this ride, you will need to let go, put your hands out in front of you and "fly." In 2000, the first flying coaster became operational, known as the *Stealth* at Paramount's Great America in Santa Clara, California. It was created by Vekoma International, and since then, you will find other flying coasters such as *Batwing* at Six Flags Over America (also created by Vekoma), and *Superman-Ultimate Flight* at Six Flags New Jersey, Great America and Georgia, created by the industry leader Bolliger and Mabillard.

Hyper/Gigi Coasters:

"Hyper coaster" was the original term given to a roller coaster that broke the two hundred-foot tall mark. The term not only applies to steel coasters, but wooden coasters as well. Most hyper coasters are non-looping, but one thing they share in common is the fact that they are very tall and extremely fast. The first one of this kind was built by Arrow Dynamics and debuted at Cedar Point in Sandusky, Ohio in May of 1989. It was called *Magnum XL-200* and stood two hundred feet above the pavement. Most hyper coasters, now "giga coasters" because they are much taller than the first hyper coasters, mimic a wood coaster design, but as you may have guessed, are hundreds of feet taller, smoother, and of course faster. The only exception to this statement can be found in a wood coaster at Paramount's Kings Island, where you will find *Son of Beast,* with a 214-foot first drop with a loop to boot, while maintaining a top speed of seventy-eight mph. What makes this so special is that the average steel hyper coaster speeds down the track at just over seventy-five mph. As hyper coasters go, if you like the feeling of your stomach in your mouth (negative g's), or the feeling of being pushed into your seat (positive g's), you will love these new monsters of the midway. They are not for the squeamish, and if you want to try these coasters, I suggest you build up your tolerance level before any attempt is ever made.

In the past few years, hyper coasters are now

Magnum XL-200 at Cedar Point in Sandusky, Ohio

Pete Trabucco

even taller than two hundred feet. *Millennium Force* at Cedar Point became the first hyper/giga coaster to stand over three hundred feet tall when it went into operation in 2000. Since then other coasters have taken that title away. Today you will find hyper coasters all over the country. Some of the most notable ones are *Titan* at Six Flags Over Texas; *Nitro* at Six Flags Great Adventure New Jersey; *Raging Bull* at Six Flags Great America in Gurnee, Illinois; and *Steel Force* at Dorney Park in Allentown, PA. There is also *Desperado* at Buffalo Bill's Resort and Casino just outside of Las Vegas, Nevada if you like to do more than just gamble.

Lately the tallest coasters, the giga coasters, have also sprung up around the country. Cedar Point's latest attraction, *Top Thrill Dragster,* shoots its passengers down the track at 120 mph and climbs to a height of 420 feet. In New Jersey you will find the tallest and fastest coaster ever created (at this writing), which races its riders around the track at 125 mph and zooms to the dizzying height of 455 feet. You will find this coaster at Six Flags Great Adventure under the name *Kingda Ka.*

Kingda Ka, Six Flags Great Adventure in New Jersey

Kingda Ka, Six Flags Great Adventure in New Jersey

Pete Trabucco

The Best Mass-Produced Coasters in the Nation!

Many people are unaware that some of the best coasters in the country (and in the world) have been mass-produced. Yes, in some cases the names have been changed at different parks, but in actuality the ride itself is exactly the same. It is just another version of a successful thrill ride that has been duplicated for the masses. Below you will see just a few of the more successful coasters that have hit our shores over the past twenty years and have been cloned all around the country. I have mentioned where you can find the best of those rides below but also list all the clones you can find around the country.

Mass-Production Model Coasters:

- *Batman the Ride* (inverted BTR) at Six Flags Great Adventure may be getting old but is still one of the best-loved inverted coasters around. True, there are many taller and faster rides in place around the country, but when you compare its size to the ride's overall intensity, sometimes bigger isn't always better. Since *Batman* was created with such a small footprint, the g-forces attained going through a particular element are in fact much higher (due to tighter turns and faster track), and this gives the ride the added oomph that we all have heard about. The ride sustains heavy g-loading (sometimes as high as five) throughout the ride and maintains a constant speed throughout. The best seats for visuals are of course the front four, but if you really want to get knocked around, and most of us do, why not try the back seats at night? There are very few lights around this ride at night, and in the evening you truly have no idea where you are going to go next. It doesn't matter how many times you ride this marvel, it will keep you second-guessing. Bolliger and Mabillard (B&M) can be very proud of this invention they concocted over a decade ago. Also worth mentioning, the queue through Gotham City while you are entering the ride itself is nicely done and accurately sets the mood for your adventure. If you can't visit New Jersey, you can find this ride also at Six Flags Magic Mountain, Six Flags Over Georgia, Six Flags Over Texas, and where the ride originated in 1992 at Six Flags Great America in Chicago.

- *Two Face the Flip Side* (vertigo style coaster) at Six Flags America in Largo, Maryland is, in a word, a pretty good ride. Named after a character from the *Batman* comic books, in this case the name is quite appropriate. The vertigo class coaster is slightly taller than its boomerang cousin (125 feet), climbing to a height of 138 feet, but what makes this coaster different is the seating arrangement. The seats are arranged so that the riders face each other, and that makes this shuttle coaster into a real winner. When you reach the top, you wait there for a few seconds and the train drops at over fifty-five miles per hour past the riders waiting in line. The first inversion is the seventy-foot boomerang, which flips you over twice. Like Vekoma's smaller cousin, the original boomerang, this element is pretty disorienting and riders experience five g's while entering it, but it's so fast, you barely even notice. After this is the loop. The train goes most of the way up the second hill, and the chain then pulls it up the rest of the way, where you wait for a few seconds. This is a good time to check out the

Pete Trabucco

people staring back at you. After another stop you go through the course in the opposite direction, streaking past the station and partially up the first hill. At this point the train is taken slowly down the hill and back to the station. It's a good ride but not overly intense, something that most of the family will be able to enjoy. Since there is only one small train running at any time, the lines will get long as the day goes by. It is best to ride this one early. If you can't ride this one you can find other vertigo coasters under the name of *Face Off* at Paramount's Kings Island, and *Invertigo* at Paramount's Great America.

- *The Sea Serpent* (boomerang style) was the first of its type ever to hit the United States. Created by Vekoma Corporation in 1984 and located out of Morey's Pier in Wildwood, New Jersey, the standard shuttle takes riders backward up to a height of 125 feet. At the top of the station, the train is released and drops through the station into a boomerang (or cobra roll) element, where

it then goes through a vertical loop and up a second lift hill. Here the train is pulled forward to the top (at 125 feet) and released backward over the same 825-foot course. The best part of this type of ride is traversing the course backward. It is quite a different experience, and one that all coaster enthusiasts ought to try. While the ride might be a little rough by today's standards, it is worth trying as long as the lines are short. Unfortunately, since only one train can be dispatched at a time, the lines tend to get pretty long on busy days. In addition to the *Sea Serpent,* here is a list of other notable boomerangs you can ride: *The Boomerang* at Knott's Berry Farm, Six Flags Fiesta Texas, and Six Flags Great Escape; *Sidewinder* at Hershey Park; *Tidal Wave* at Trimper's Rides; and *Mind Eraser* at Six Flags Worlds of Adventure. In addition to those mentioned, you can find three dozen more of these shuttle coasters all over the world, making them the most common mass-production model coaster ever created.

- *The Great Nor'Easter* (suspended looping coaster, or SLC, commonly classified as an inverted coaster) at Morey's Pier in Wildwood, New Jersey may be a standard Vekoma coaster, but through its location it gives riders a great ride for their money. This coaster is built literally out on the pier itself, so when you are at the top of this lift hill, you see nothing but blue sky and ocean in front of you. That is, of course, until you begin to dive to the right toward the pier below at speeds of fifty-five miles per hour. You don't always get a smooth ride on the *Great Nor'Easter*, but depending on the day, and like catching the perfect wave, if you hit it just right, you will get a pretty intense ride. The *Nor'Easter* seats two abreast in trains that carry the older horse-collar restraints. A few of its struts were changed on this ride, as was the station itself, and now it wraps itself around one the best water flumes on the east coast. The clearances are very tight, and you find yourself raising your legs as high as possible as you ride this SLC coaster.

This SLC possesses five inversions: a cobra roll that inverts the riders twice; a twist loop; and two heart line flips. I consider this ride one of the best of the dozen or so SLC coasters that Vekoma has erected in North America. Some of the other Vekoma SLC coasters can be found at Six Flags America, Six Flags New England, Six Flags Darien Lake, and Elitch Gardens. You can also find the coaster under other names, such as *Serial Thriller* at Six Flags Worlds of Adventure.

- *The Crazy Mouse* (spinning type coaster) created by Reverchon takes the wild mouse ride to the next level. Like the wild mouse, this ride goes up a lift hill and is sent down the track with hairpin turns and small drops that increase as you go along. But during the second level, the four-passenger car/mice spin freely during the ride, instead of always facing forward. This concept spins the cars (like a Virginia wheel) giving this compact 1377-foot long coaster tremendous punch when the cars reach the lower level. The *Crazy Mouse* on the famous Steel Pier in Atlantic City stands forty-nine feet high with one thirty-foot drop and was the first wild mouse to be created in North America. Originally, this coaster stood at Dinosaur Beach in Wildwood (in 1997) and was moved to the Atlantic City's famous pier in 1999. The view of all AC's boardwalk hotels from this ride makes this an experience one to remember. Currently, there are twenty-four crazy mouse coasters around the world. Some other notable coasters in the United States are *Crazy Mouse* at Motor World in Virginia Beach; *Crazy Mouse* at Myrtle Beach; *Primeval Whirl* at Disney World's Animal Kingdom and the *Exterminator* at Kennywood Park.

• *The Python* (zyclon loop) at Playland in Ocean City, New Jersey is just one of sixteen zyclon loops created worldwide by Italian based company Pinfari Corporation. What I like about this one is that you get a good ride from start to finish. It is definitely the ride to choose if you are just starting and want to try loops. Standing at thirty-six feet high and racing down the 1200-foot long track, I have found that you get a pleasant experience all the way. Being at the Jersey shore and overlooking the Atlantic Ocean is also a definite plus on this ride. Usually this type of model has two four-seat cars attached to it, but be careful. The lap bars are pretty snug, and if you are an adult you might want to hold in your stomach to get in. Even though there is a loop here, this coaster is definitely in the family coaster category, and one that parents should try with their kids.

If you like this one then you may be ready for the next level of coaster thrills. This coaster is actually a progression from other Pinfari non-looping coasters of the same name which came before it. In fact there are only three of these babies in the United States. You can find the other two under the name of *Looping Star* at the Pier Rides in Ocean City, Maryland, or at Beech Bend in Bowling Green, Kentucky.

- *The Runaway Train* (mine train style) at Six Flags Great Adventure in New Jersey isn't the oldest mine train (that accolade goes to *Mine Train* at Six Flags Over Texas circa 1966), nor is the tallest or fastest of the two dozen plus Arrow Corporation mine trains currently in operation. What I can say is that in my mind, it's simply one of the best. Built in 1974 and the first roller coaster to be built at this park, the *Runaway Train* is 2400 feet long (a mine train standard), utilizes only one lift hill (seventy feet high), and races its guests around the track in excess of thirty-five miles per hour. Its scenic views of the park are spectacular, and that last swooping (and most photographed) turn over a manmade lake is what separates this mine train from all others. Recommended for the advancing beginner coaster aficionado, this is indeed a family coaster with a capital "F."

A mine train coaster is designed to create the feel of an old runaway train. It usually features sharp turns and short little bunny hops. The train itself looks like a string of coal mining cars, and in most cases you can find mini locomotives right up front. Except for the tunnels, *Runaway Train* has all these elements. Along the way, you will usually encounter tunnels and mineshafts as you go. One observation I did make about *Runaway Train* was if you have small children, it is highly recommended that you make sure your child is a little taller than the minimum height restriction of forty-eight inches. The restraints are old and have a little play in them. I have seen some really small passengers almost eject from their seats at times, so please use good judgment here. Other mine trains to look for in America are *Adventure Express* at Paramount's Kings Island, *Cedar Creek Mine Ride* at Cedar Point, *Goldrusher* at Six Flags Magic Mountain, *Thunder Express* at Dollywood, *Traiblazer* at Hershey Park, and Arrow's latest mine train creation, *Canyon Blaster* at Six Flags Great Escape. Mine trains are also being produced by Morgan Manufacturing Company, as there is currently a renewed interest in building this type of classic coaster.

- *The Wildcat* coaster at Keansburg Amusement Park in New Jersey is a great ride for beginners as well as experienced coaster enthusiasts. Created by Anton Schwarzkopf, this coaster might only be 50-feet high, but its figure eight design and high visibility seating arrangement (usually just one car that looks like a German-style automobile) make this a decent ride for your local amusement park. The cars seem to glide at times as they traverse each end of the 1380-foot structure. But what makes the *Wildcat* a classic Schwarzkopf coaster is the three steep drops of over forty feet that will treat the rider to some unexpected negative g's and do it at speeds approaching forty miles per hour. A welcome for all those who need to feel the rush, the *Wildcat* can be a little rough at times for its smaller passengers. Overall, it delivers a good ride experience for its size. There are three versions of the *Wildcat* that have been produced in the past of which this one (at Keansberg) is the largest at 50 feet in height. Is this a state of the art thrill ride? Of course not, but for its size it is an A-1 family coaster, and one that still has a lot of mileage left on it. Overall you will find over twenty of these coasters worldwide. You can also find the *Wildcat* under the same name at Cedar Point, in Sandusky, Ohio; Jolly Roger Amusement Park in Ocean City, Maryland; Martin's Fantasy Island in Grand Island, New York; William's Grove Park in Mechanicsburg, PA, and under the names of Williamsburg; *Cyclone* at Sandspit Cavendish Beach in Canada; and *Rails* at Valley Fair Park in Shakopee, Minnesota.

- *Python* (corkscrew style) in my mind was the best example of this type of coaster ever built. Standing at seventy feet in height, the *Python* sends its riders into a tight right turn, followed by a sixty-five-foot drop into a double corkscrew. Be careful not to touch the trees as you go through these elements. The ride comes close enough to the foliage that you feel like you can grab a few tree leaves as you go by. Reaching speeds of forty miles per hour, this coaster rides along a 1250-foot track that you only wish were just a bit longer. But back in 1977, this coaster was state of the art and one of only a few coasters that took their riders upside down.

In fact, *Python* was one of the first modern coasters to invert passengers. The first coaster to do this is still in operation and can be found at Silverwood Theme Park in Athol, ID as *Corkscrew.* Coaster aficionados might recall that Arrow came up with this design way back in 1975. I like this coaster type because it was the first coaster I ever rode that took me upside down. "You never forget your first!" It can thrill newer-generation riders even today and was my first choice for those who have braved the family coaster genre and want to experience inversion in its simplest form.

Overall, there are less than a dozen of these Arrow coasters operating around the world. There are only three left (now that Python is gone) in current operation in the United States. You can find the other two under the names of *Corkscrew* at Michigan Adventure in Muskegon, MI and *Canobie Corkscrew* at Canobie Lake Park in Salem, New Hampshire.

- *The Jet Star* series was Anton Schwarzkopf's first portable coaster design and features straight and steep drops with high-speed, banked turns as you fly down the 1700-foot track. Currently there are just five permanent *Jet Star* coasters running in the United States. I like the *Jet Star, Jet Star II* (which had a longer track), and its bigger brother *Jumbo Jet* because they always seem to give you a great ride and are able to accomplish this in a very small space. The last version of this coaster was the *City Jet* (a smaller version of the *Jumbo Jet*) and like *Jumbo Jet* utilized a spiral lift hill and an electric motor housed inside the car that took its passengers up the lift hill. You can find the *Jet Star* at Thrill Ville, USA in Turner, OR, and under the name of *Tig'rr Coaster* at Indiana Beach, Indiana. A dark version (and one of the best currently running) can be found under the name *Nightmare at Crack Axle Canyon* at Six Flags Great Escape in upstate New York. Only one *Jet Star II* is currently running, at Lagoon in Farmington, UT. My favorite *Jumbo Jet* version (only three running in the world) can be seen at the Coney Island Boardwalk in Brooklyn, New York. I am told that this ride was temporarily closed due to problems with its trains.

- *City Jet* at Gillian's Wonderland Pier in Ocean City, New Jersey is the only one of its kind left in North America. In fact there were only a handful of these coasters ever built around the entire world. The *City Jet* is located on the Ocean City boardwalk (in Gillian's) overlooking the Atlantic Ocean, and from the lift hill you can literally see the many hotels of Atlantic City in the distance. Originally located at Shaheen's Fun-O-Rama in Salisbury Beach, Massachusetts, the coaster moved to this boardwalk location in 1976. A smaller version of the *Jet Star* series, coaster *City Jet* utilizes a spiral lift hill. An electric motor is housed inside the car and takes its passengers up thirty-six feet before it drops them one foot short of the ground along 1362 feet of track. Built by the Schwarzkopf Company, this coaster is great for those who are just starting out on their coaster careers or for those parents who want to see if they can still ride the rails. It is a pleasant coaster to ride, and one that everyone in the family can enjoy.

- *The Flitzer* at Morey's Pier in Wildwood represents just one of half a dozen permanent coasters that currently operate around the world. Personally, I think this one is the best of the bunch! It was first created as a portable coaster by Franz Schwarzkopf (Anton's brother) and sold by the Zierer Company, known for their seventy-five Tivoli coasters around the world. *The Flitzer* at Morey's Pier, first built in 1981, takes its passengers (overlooking the ocean, of course) to a height of twenty-five feet. Passengers are then subjected to a slew of zippy turns and twists all through the 1200-foot course. Passengers usually sit together in a line, sort of like a log flume arrangement, and the more weight you have in each single car, the faster you will go. This is an excellent starter coaster for anyone who wants to try coasters and is perfect for the kids. If you live in New Jersey, you will find three of six of these coasters right along the Jersey shoreline. They all go under the same name, *Flitzer,* and are located at Jenkinson's Family Center in Point Pleasant; Keansburg Amusement Park in Keansburg; and Playland in Ocean City, New Jersey. Another notable *Flitzer* can be found at the Ocean City Pier Rides in Ocean City, Maryland.

- *The Wild Mouse* coaster at Hershey Park, PA, is my top choice for this type of ride. This isn't a very easy selection to make, since there are literally two dozen of these coasters operating all over the United States. If you find yourself in a decent amusement park, chances are there will be a wild mouse ride in the park. But every once in a while you find a coaster that is far and away better than all the others in the same classification. In my mind (and I have not ridden every wild mouse coaster in the country), that coaster is located in central Pennsylvania. Standing at fifty feet over its entrance, and as it was built on the side of a hill, over eighty feet high on the other side, this attraction is the best of the best. You definitely notice the difference in height as you are going over the edge on that one side. It will definitely wake you up. Built by Mack Corporation in 1999, *Wild Mouse* at times has intense tight turns and gives you that out of control feeling as you move along the 1200 feet of track. Take my word for it, hats and glasses off for this one! I almost don't even want to call this a family coaster, even though it is.

The wild mouse concept is a simple but ingenious one—Create a single car train on a track with very, very tight turns. Position the car wheels closer to the rear of the car than on a traditional coaster, causing the front of the car to travel past each turn before suddenly U-turning, making the riders feel that their car is literally going to fall off the track. If you are able to achieve this sensation, then you have been successful. They have done this at Hershey Park. But not just there! Wild mouse coasters have been popular since the 1950s and '60 s, but lately you will find many new ones popping up just about everywhere. So popular are these rides right now that you will find many coaster companies currently creating these popular rides. Coaster companies like Arrow, Mack, Maurer, Miler, Schiff, and Sohne have thrown their hat in the ring on producing these coasters. Some are better than others, but they all manage to get you and your family's adrenaline going in a small amount of space. They do mine! Other wild mouse rides of note can be found at Casino Pier, Seaside, New Jersey; Cedar Point in Sandusky, Ohio; Dorney Park in Allentown, Pennsylvania; Kennywood Park, West Miffin, Pennsylvania; Jolly Rodger Amusement Park, Ocean City, Maryland; Playland Park in Ocean City, New Jersey; *Wilde Maus* at Busch Gardens in Virginia; and *Mad Mouse* at Michigan Adventure, Muskegon, Michigan.

Top Roller Coaster Manufacturers

Ever wonder who creates the amusement park rides that we love so much? Well, this section is dedicated to those professionals who work so diligently to get their product to us. They are the ones who bend the laws of physics and make the impossible possible. They are the ones who make this industry what it is today. For the excitement they bring to us, this publication would not be complete without giving them a holler. For those who sometimes fear coasters, again it is good to know who makes what ride and where you can find the thrill that won't scare your pants off too much!

Roller Coaster Corporation of America (RCCA):

This company is based out of Atlanta. Over the years, this group has created some of the best wooden roller coasters we have seen. Six Flags Over Georgia's *Great American Scream Machine* was created by this company and still is a thrill for riders today. Famed designer John Allen created a masterpiece when he built this ride back in 1973. One of their best wooden coasters ever built is at Paramount's Kings Island amusement park in Ohio. It is there that you will find the only modern looping *wood* roller coaster in *Son of Beast*. Recently this company has teamed up with Togo Corporation to create some wild wood rides in Japan. If you like rides that are innovative but not overwhelming, then this company is for you.

Great Coasters International (GCI):

In 1996, this company was created by roller coaster designers Michael Boodley and Clair Haine, Jr. One of the most famous rides they concocted can be found at Hershey Park with the name *The Wildcat*. You can also find a super wood coaster at Six Flags America, *Roar*. They also created a classic race coaster at Busch Gardens Tampa named *Gwazi*, which I hope you get the chance to ride. They are the designers as well of what I feel is the best racing coaster out there when in 2000, they built *Lightning Racer* (LR), also located at Hershey Park in Hershey, Pennsylvania. Overall, if you love swooping turns and crazy maze-like courses, you will love their stuff. If you are like me and want speed mixed in with that out of control feeling, and heart-pounding action, their racers (especially *LR*) are the best of the bunch.

Custom Coaster International (CCI):

Many of the classic wooden roller coasters we ride today have been created by this company. All you have to do is ride one of their coasters to know that these guys are the best in the business. Ranging from smaller but enjoyable coasters, such as the *Sky Princess* at Dutch Wonderland in Lancaster, Pennsylvania, to their best works *The Raven, Shivering Timbers, Rampage,* and one of my all-time favorites, *Ghostrider* (all listed in my top woodie section), you can't improve on perfection. Ladies and gentlemen, when you add their classic, *The Texas Giant,* to their collection, you can't help but see perfection in all their works. For those who love classic lines on rides that vary like the people who ride them, look for the name CCI and you are truly in for an incredible ride experience.

Arrow Dynamics of California:

Arrow Dynamics is one of the oldest roller coaster companies around (1946), and the first to use steel in their work. Founded by Ed Morgan and Karl Bacon, this company started out with a small park that they owned and built into a roller coaster empire. Then in 1955, a man named Walt approached them to do the impossible. The idea was to build not a wooden roller coaster, but one made of steel. This coaster would run down a mountain that he found so appealing. The ride would take people in and out of the mountain on its journey down the first-ever steel track. That ride still exists today, and ever since its completion in 1959, the *Matterhorn Bobsleds* at Disneyland (Walt's place); California has been thrilling young and old riders for decades. Arrow also created such classic attractions as *Pirates of the Caribbean, Dumbo, Peter Pan's Flight,* the *Haunted Mansion* and countless others for the Disney Corporation. As far as coasters go, there are literally too many creations to name. Chances are your local amusement park has one of their rides today. One of Arrow's best, however, can be found at Cedar Point under the name *Magnum XL 200*. This 205-foot marvel once held records and is still the standard by which all mega coasters are measured. Indeed, without Arrow Corporation, the modern-day amusement park concept would never have existed.

Premier Rides Corporation:

Based out of Millerville, Maryland, this company has again set a new bar for the roller coaster industry. They have incorporated a new propulsion system called Linear Induction Motors, or LIM. The concept is bold and daring. Why not take your standard coaster and get rid of the lift hill? Why not start the ride off like you were an airplane blasting off an aircraft carrier? Go from 0 to sixty, seventy, or eighty mph in seconds, using magnets to get the job done. This company was so innovative, even NASA took an interest in these coaster designs for use in their space programs. Some coasters of note are

Flight of Fear (Maryland and Ohio), *Jokers Jinx, Mr. Freeze* (Texas and St. Louis), and *The Ride* in Las Vegas, Nevada. Their best work to date can be found at Six Flags Great Adventure in Jackson, New Jersey, with *Batman and Robin-the Chiller*. Most recently the company is marketing new combination flume and roller coaster rides with the invention of *Buzzsaw Falls* in Missouri's Silver Dollar City. The company was founded by Jim Seay and is looked upon as an innovative company that creates extreme (with a big X) rides to the public.

Bolliger and Mabillard (B&M):

Bolliger and Mabillard are people who created several new concepts for the roller coaster enthusiast. Their coasters are known for the extreme elements they create, but are also known for how smooth these rides can be throughout the course. Walter Bolliger and Claude Mabillard knew what they were doing when they created the classic *Batman and Robin* inverted coaster in 1992. Since then, these coasters have popped up almost everywhere. Known for their smooth but high-g ride environment, these coasters set the standard for all inverted coasters to follow. B&M also created the first floorless coaster concept, which even today elicits thrills and chills in everyone who rides them. The roller coasters *Medusa* (Six Flags Great Adventure) and *Kraken* (SeaWorld Florida) exemplify the best of these roller coasters. B&M also excel in steel mega coasters like *Nitro* and *Apollo's Chariot* (on my top steel coaster list) and still have much more planned for us in the future. Even though this company is still in relative infancy (as compared to others), B&M can boast over forty rides in place and operating around the world in just the last fifteen years. An impressive statistic for such a young but innovative company.

Giovanola Corporation:

Joseph Giovanola founded this company in 1888 (you read it correctly), but it took over one hundred years to get into the roller coaster business. The Switzerland-based company has two very dominating coasters in the market today. They are almost exact duplicates of each other but go under different names, *Goliath* at Six Flags Magic Mountain California and *Titan* at Six Flags Over Texas. Both are great rides. Not only are they tall (255 feet), they both offer high, sustained positive-g forces on a rider that no other coaster can match. If you don't like the feeling of being pinned to your chair for a sustained period of time (like an astronaut on takeoff) this type of ride is not for you. I see real promise in their two-place and four-place seating designs and look forward to their latest concoctions.

Interman AG of Switzerland:

Like B&M and Giovanola, these guys are based out of Switzerland. Unlike the others mentioned, they have created not just the best steel coasters the world has seen, but wooden ones as well. Working for years in association with the Schwarzkopf Company, some of the great steel coasters of the 70s were built by Interman. One of their best mega steel coasters is the *Superman Series Ride of Steel* coaster, which has been ranked in the top ten coasters for many years. They also created the first looping steel coaster in 1976, with the coaster *Revolution* which still operates today at Six Flags Magic Mountain in Valencia, California. Interman works with every style of coaster and most recently is working on linear induction powered and unparalleled steel drop towers that simply boggle your mind and senses. The two tallest coasters on the planet belong to this company, *Kingda Ka* and *Top Thrill Dragster*. They are hydraulic launch coasters (the Navy uses them to launch their planes off carriers) and they fly down the track at upwards of 120 mph, topping the sky at over 450 feet. As good as those coasters are, Interman AG will always be the company that brought me to the best steel roller coaster every created. That coaster still is one of the best in the world, and at over three hundred feet tall is still one of the tallest. The ride? *Millennium Force* at Cedar Point in Sandusky, Ohio. Need I say more!

DH Morgan Manufacturing Company:

Dana Morgan, cofounder of DH Morgan, has a lot to be thankful for. This company started out delivering roller coaster components and trains; and has progressed to become one of the best around. In the mid-1990's it built two 200-foot mega coasters that really put Morgan on the map: *Wild Thing* at Minnesota's Valleyfair and *Steel Force* at Dorney Park (one of my favorites) in Pennsylvania. Another coaster, *Mamba,* at Missouri's Worlds of Fun solidified their place in the roller coaster industry. In 1999, they built what at the time was the tallest coaster ever, *Steel Dragon 2000,* and is now part of Chance Morgan Coasters, Inc. Still, with all they have done, one of my favorite rides from this company isn't the tallest nor the fastest. It is *Steel Eel* at SeaWorld San Antonio, possibly one the most aesthetically pleasing (that means beautiful) coasters ever created.

S and S Power Inc.:

Stan Checketts is the founder of this company and has put himself on the map with the roller coasters he has built. In 1994, Stan and his wife created S and S Power, and all those famous drop and space shot towers you have been riding over the years are theirs. Since then they have created rides such as *Hypersonic XLC* and now have created a way to propel rides from the vertical to the horizontal using compressed air. Their innovation was the beginning of the biggest and best coasters we have on the planet today.

Vekoma International Corporation:

Vekoma by far has more roller coaster installations in the past twenty-five years than any other company, topping over one hundred at the time of this writing. Founded in 1926 in the Netherlands, this company did not become involved in the roller coaster industry until the 1960's. In my mind, the Vekoma Company was the sole creator of the boomerang series of coasters that were so popular in the 1980s. They also created their own version of the inverted coaster (their answer to B&M's *Batman* series), which tends to be a little rough on your back, but nonetheless is a great ride. Most recently they have gotten into LIM style coasters, with one of their most famous being located at Walt Disney World's MGM studios. It goes by the name *Rock n' Roller Coaster* and is one of the best dark ride coasters that you will find. I should also mention that Vekoma created for Universal Studios a first-rate aquatic ride called *Jurassic Park, The Ride* at Universal's Islands Of Adventure in Florida. Finally, this company stands alone in that it was the first (maybe not the most popular) company to introduce the Flying Dutchman (flying) coaster concept which other companies are currently using today. Indeed, Vekoma is a steady player in the roller coaster market and hopefully will continue to manufacture more innovative rides for us roller coaster enthusiasts in the near future.

Anton Schwarzkopf Corporation:

You can't mention companies that had a great influence on the industry without mentioning Anton Schwarzkopf. His work for Zierer and Interman puts him high on the roller coaster design list. You will find his coaster designs all over the world; chances are you have ridden one of these coasters in the past. Schwarzkopf had a way of creating intense rides in small spaces. If you compare them to today's extravagant coasters, you might be disappointed, but remember, his coasters were created for a different world, and I can bet you any amount of money that right next to today's tallest and fastest coasters, you will find a Schwarzkopf *Jet Star* or *Wildcat* roller coaster.

Togo Corporation:

This company has been Japan's foremost thrill ride supplier for the past fifteen years. Togo has been in the amusement park industry for many years, creating some of the best Ferris wheels, dark rides and kiddy coasters around. In 1984, Togo hit the US market with *King Cobra*—a stand-up coaster for Paramount's Kings Island. Several years later, they created *Ultra Twister* at Six Flags Astroland. One of their best coasters in the United States is *Manhattan Express* at New York, New York Hotel and Casino, in Las Vegas, Nevada. Togo Corporation boasts over fifty roller coasters worldwide and is the prime inventor of the heart line roll element used in their attractions.

America's Top Steel Roller Coasters

There are literally thousands of coasters in the country. So how do you pick the best ones to ride? Well, there are many ways to accomplish this. You can rely on surveys or just go on what the rider attendance has been over a certain time period. When I decide which coaster to ride, I take a simpler approach. I simply ask myself if I will enjoy this ride, and afterwards, would I go on it again? If the answer is yes, then it was a great ride and one that I would recommend to others. After all, in the grand scheme of things, the deciding factor on whether a ride is successful or not is its overall excitement and re-ride ability. I can safely say that if you ask one hundred people what their favorite wood or steel coasters are (and I have), you will surely get results that are swayed by where the rider lives, his level of

enthusiasm, and what he/she is looking for in a thrill ride. Some enthusiasts love steep drops from dizzying heights. Others prefer speed but hate inversions. Still others love inversions but hate lengthy drops from high towers. The combinations of criteria can go on and on. One person's thrilling ride experience can be another person's nightmare, so the trick here is to find an experience that everyone will enjoy. In my mind, that is the key to building the ultimate roller coaster. Variety is the spice of life, so would it be any different when it comes to riding roller coasters?

Having said that, I can easily say that my top thirty roller coaster (for both wood and steel) picks are based on my experiences and personal preferences, as well as interviews with hundreds of other riders. From all the information I have gathered, I have come up with my top thirty steel and wood roller coasters in the nation. Please use this guide to help you decide which coasters you would like to experience, but in the end please remember, it is ultimately your own opinion that really counts. Enjoy!

1. *Millennium Force* at Cedar Point, Sandusky, Ohio.

2. *Superman-Ride of Steel* (now called Bizarro) at Six Flags New England.

3. *Apollo's Chariot* at Busch Gardens, Williamsburg, Virginia.

4. *KingDa Ka* at Six Flags Great Adventure, Jackson, New Jersey.

5. *Montu* at Busch Gardens, Tampa, Florida.

6. *Nitro* at Six Flags Great Adventure, Jackson, New Jersey.

7. *Top Thrill Dragster* at Cedar Point, Sandusky, Ohio.

8. *Volcano-The Blast Coaster* at Paramount's Kings Dominion, Virginia.

9. *The Incredible Hulk* at Universal Studio's Islands of Adventure, Florida.

10. *Medusa* at Six Flags Great Adventure, Jackson, New Jersey.

11. *Griffin* at Busch Gardens Williamsburg, Virginia

12. *Phantom's Revenge* at Kennywood in West Miffin, Pennsylvania.

13. *Superman-Ride of Steel* at Six Flags America, Largo, Maryland.

14. *Raptor* at Cedar Point, Sandusky, Ohio.

15. *Superman the Ultimate Flight*-Six Flags, Atlanta, Georgia.

16. *Kumba* at Busch Gardens, Tampa, Florida.

17. *Titan* at Six Flags Over Texas, Arlington, Texas.

18. *Dueling Dragons* at Universal Studios Islands of Adventure, Florida.

19. *X2* at Six Flags Magic Mountain, Valencia, California.

20. *Steel Force* at Dorney Park, Allentown, Pennsylvania.

21. *Kraken* at SeaWorld, Florida.

22. *Alpengeist* at Busch Gardens, Williamsburg, Virginia.

23. *Riddler's Revenge* at Six Flags Magic Mountain, Valencia, California.

24. *Hypersonic XLC* at Paramount's King's Dominion, Virginia.

25. *Great Bear* at Hershey Park, Pennsylvania.

26. *Batman the Dark Knight* at Six Flags New England, Agawon, Massachusetts.

27. *Batwing* at Six Flags America, Largo, Maryland.

28. *Expedition Everest* at Disney's Animal Kingdom in Orlando, Florida.

29. *Rock n Roller Coaster* at Disney's MGM studios, Florida.

30. *Maverick* at Cedar Point in Sandusky Ohio.

1 *Millennium Force* at Cedar Point, Sandusky, Ohio has truly changed any preconception of how high a roller coaster can be safely built. At a height of 310 feet, with over-banked turns of 122 degrees, this steel marvel is a sight to see and can be observed for miles in any direction from the park. Built by Interman AG Corporation at a cost of $25 million, *Millennium Force* broke all the record books in 2000 and has one of the fastest lift hills to boot. You travel up this hill at around fourteen miles per hour and reach the top in seconds (not in minutes as you do on most mega type coasters), which can be a good thing if you hate to linger at great heights. Once at the top, the view is incredible, but it is that first drop that makes *Millennium* a cut above the rest. I assure you that it will take your breath away. Traveling at speeds of over ninety miles per hour and dropping at an eighty-degree angle, you will be moved by the negative g's of this ride. But that will only be the beginning of a memorable experience on *Millennium Force.* This ride is simply a ride of dizzying heights followed by a consistent high-

Millennium Force at Cedar Point, Sandusky, Ohio

Pete Trabucco

Millennium Force at Cedar Point, Sandusky, Ohio

speed trek throughout the 6500-foot track, topped off with three of the tallest hills you will ever find. And let's not forget those over-banked turns! Also on *Millennium Force,* you will experience dramatic tunnels and take a ride on a very sleek two-across stadium seat train that gives a smooth but rapid ride throughout. The way I see it, if you like continual drops and a lot of airtime, then *Superman Ride of Steel* at Six Flags New England is your top coaster. But if you want the best first drop in the nation, along with sheer overall speed and highly banked turns, then *Millennium* is your choice as the best of the best. I personally love them both.

On the down side, even though *Millenium Force* is no longer the tallest coaster around, lines for this ride are also out of this world. It is best to try this ride just as the park opens and stay close with the crowd. You can also get in an hour early if you stay at one of the hotels at Cedar Point. If you attempt it during the midday hours, it is almost a foregone conclusion that you will spend most of your day waiting in line for this world-class coaster. One note of caution:

Millennium has one of the strictest ride enforcement rules around. Your seatbelt must be securely fastened with at least half an inch leeway in order to experience the force. Those individuals who have over a 44-inch waist might not be allowed to ride.

2 *Superman—Ride of Steel* (now called Bizarro) at Six Flags New England is truly a coaster in a league of its own. Manufactured by Interman AG of Switzerland, *Superman—Ride of Steel* shares its namesake with others hypercoasters of similar technical proportions located under the same name in New York and in Maryland, but this ride is certainly *no* clone of the others. This latest version is truly airtime coaster heaven for all who ride her and truly is a dream machine. In 2003 *Superman—Ride of Steel* took its rightful place as "the best coaster on the planet," according to *Amusement Today Magazine.* It accomplished this after a couple of years holding the second place slot behind *Millennium Force* at Cedar Point. Yes, *Millennium Force* is one great ride, but even the *Force* cannot boast the amount of airtime

Pete Trabucco

(or floating time) that *Ride of Steel* delivers in one seating. *Superman* also features an incredible lift hill, rising slowly alongside the Connecticut River. This breathtaking view from the top only heightens the level of excitement, as the train climbs to just over 208 feet. From here, you can enjoy the view and note that on a clear day, you can see for ten miles around. However, you will only experience the view for a brief moment before plummeting down the first hill at almost eighty mph. You should be prepared for two and a half minutes of pure, unchecked adrenaline running through your veins throughout the ride. From the seventy plus degree, 221-foot first drop, to those absolutely amazing eighty-five-foot bunny hops, it's truly a thrill a second. You literally feel like you are going to be ejected out of your seat on almost every hill, but fortunately with those comfortable and very effective waist harnesses, there is no need for a parachute on this ride.

In addition to the negative drops and the feeling of being ejected from your seat, there is so much more to this ride! When you enter the two tunnels, you will experience cold spots that can't be found anywhere else. In a word, it's "Cold in them there tunnels," and the fog makes for multiple sensations not usually experienced so intensely on other rides. To finish up your ride, there is one more surprise in store for you. The rider ends his adventure with an incredible, high g-force dual helix finale. Not bad at all! It's one of the best I have ridden, and I am sure you will think so as well! Note that the lines can be really long on this one, so make this your first stop when entering the park. If, however, you have to wait a while, take it from me, the ride is still worth it. *Superman—Ride of Steel* at Six Flags New England is truly a coaster that all other mega coasters must measure themselves against, and in my mind is truly a cut above the rest. What a ride!

3 *Apollo's Chariot* at Busch Gardens, Williamsburg, Virginia was ranked in the top just a few years ago, but don't let that information sway your decision. After riding it several times, I can see why it is a true favorite! If you are a coaster fanatic, this is your sole reason to visit this park. Highlighted by an impressive 210-foot first drop, this ride features great floating time and high negative g's on almost every hill. The out and back design was the first of three mega coasters created by Bolliger and Mabillard. (*Raging Bull* at Six Flags Great America and *Nitro* at Six Flags Great Adventure would complete the package a few years later.) The ride makes excellent use of the park's natural valleys, with three drops skimming the "Rhine River." The turning drop to the left on the third hill is one of the best I have seen. It is safe to say that Bolliger and Mabillard really took the time to make this ride work.

All told, there are nine drops on this coaster, and if you measured all the drops together, it would total 825 feet, a world record for coasters when it was first created. On *Apollo's Chariot,* every seat is enjoyable. This ride is very fast and can be intense, reaching seventy-five miles per hour at times but is never over the edge. You will also experience one of the most comfortable rolling stock trains ever created. If you don't like hypercoasters (coasters two hundred feet and higher), then *Chariot* might just change your mind about them. It did for my wife, who absolutely hates long straight drops. All the pieces certainly do fit together in this presentation to create a fantastic, enjoyable, and fun ride experience for all who ride.

4 *Kingda Ka* at Six Flags Great Adventure in Jackson, New Jersey is not just the biggest and fastest coaster in the world… It's also the baddest! *Kingda Ka,* the newest ride at Six Flags, stands more than forty-five stories tall at 456 feet—roughly three times the height of the Statue of Liberty—and propels riders at speeds of approximately 130 mph in less than four seconds. This is more than fifty-five mph faster than the *Batman and Robin* roller coaster and forty-five mph faster than the beloved *Nitro* also located at the Jackson, New Jersey park. In addition, the ride's fall is performed at a 270-degree angle spiral, corkscrewing riders as they descend at record-breaking speeds. When *Kingda Ka* opened in 2005, the coaster broke all the records. What if a coaster

Pete Trabucco

could be launched at 128 miles per hour in just a few seconds, be catapulted to the dizzying height of 450 feet, plummet down at 120 mph hour and still be back to the starting gate in less than 30 seconds. Well the manufacturer (B&M) came up a ride that would do all of these things and much more. *Kinda Ka* is very similar to another powerhouse ride called *Top Thrill Dragster* but unlike *Top Thrill,* you never know when you are going to be rocketed down the 3,118 foot long track and at the end of *Kingda Ka;* get ready for a 130 foot hill that will literally pull you out of your seat. At the top of this last hill, you will experience zero gravity and know what it feels like to be in outer space if only for a second or two. All in all, *Kingda Ka* is an experience you must not miss and make sure you wear some eye protection. At these speeds you will need it.

5 *Montu* at Busch Gardens, Tampa, Florida is one the best inverted coasters I have ever ridden. Nestled in the Egyptian section of the park, the coaster really does fit well into its en-vironment. *Montu* was built by Bolliger and Mabillard (B&M) and opened back in 1996 as the world's tallest inverted coaster at 150 feet. It was also the first inverted coaster to up the inversion level to seven, and the inversions are truly worth it. They come very quickly, so try not to close your eyes during the ride. On the first drop, please take note of the crocodile pit (if you can see it) that appears directly beneath you. After that experience, you can expect *Montu* to take its passenger through tunnels, around temples and through a few excavation ditches that you swear will leave your body in pieces.

Yet the best part of this ride comes during the second half of *Montu's* run. When you think the worst is over, you are hit with several tight inversions where you swear you are going to hit the walls all around you. This part of the ride is strangely reminiscent of another ride, *Big Bad Wolf* at Busch Gardens' sister park in Williamsburg, Virginia. On the *Wolf,* you get to maneuver quite closely through a Bavarian village, but on *Montu* the ride takes you through a Middle Eastern setting instead. As in all inverted coasters, I suggest the front seat for the best visuals and the very back for that out of control sensation. It's a great ride but not recommended for the faint of heart.

6 *Nitro* at Six Flags Great Adventure is without a doubt one of the most intense rides I have ever been on. From its 215-foot steep dive (the tallest B&M coaster to date) to the high g turnaround (helix) section, it is a ride that you will not soon forget. Bolliger and Mabillard do it again with a coaster that is consistently ranked no less than fifth in the world by *Amusement Today Magazine,* and it is safe to say that *Nitro* is more than just your average hypercoaster! It's an elite machine among elite machines! And although its L-shaped out and back layout borrows plenty from *Apollo's Chariot,* this monster has some new tricks up its sleeves. At sixty-six degrees, the angle of the first descent is far from completely vertical, but from this dizzying height, it sure feels like it could be. In addition to its first drop, *Nitro* has plenty of secondary drops, turns, and high-speed maneuvers that will literally keep you guessing.

I am amazed that no matter how many times I ride this coaster, there is a different element that shocks and amazes me each time, and even though it delivers a consistent ride, no two are exactly alike. The best seat on this ride is the left front seat. The reason for this occurs on *Nitro's* second drop: A 189-foot plunge to the left leaves the unsuspecting passenger stationed in that seat looking straight down at the ground below, while racing at speeds in excess of eighty mph. On the way up the lift hills, riders will notice signs which point out how high you are in comparison to famous structures around the world, such marvels as the Sphinx in Egypt (sixty-six feet), Niagara Falls (176 feet), and the Statue of Liberty (189 feet). Overall, the ride is extremely smooth, fast and airtime-filled. Clearly one of the best and most intense rides at Great Adventure (along with *Kingda Ka*), but watch out for those lines. They can be pretty long at times. This needs to be your first or second stop as you enter the park!

Top Thrill Dragster at Cedar Point in Sandusky, Ohio

7 *Top Thrill Dragster* at Cedar Point in Sandusky, Ohio is in a class all by itself. Riders begin their epic journey aboard this whopping forty-two-story screamer by securing themselves into ultra-cool trains that resemble top fuel dragsters. The train then moves into a "starting line" position, where it is launched forward, reaching 120 mph in approximately four seconds. The train then zooms straight up the 420-foot-tall hill on track that rotates ninety degrees, crests the coaster's apex and then free falls back to Earth. But hold on, this isn't your father's roller coaster. As the train races four hundred feet to the ground, the track twists an unbelievable 270 degrees—what a rush! Riders then return to the station to begin regaling their friends with stories of the greatest ride of their lives. Designed by world-renowned coaster manufacturer Intamin AG of Wollerau, Switzerland, *Top Thrill Dragster* is located directly between two other Cedar Point legends: the Magnum XL-200 and Millennium Force roller coasters. Top Thrill Dragster was voted an impressive number ten in

Top Thrill Dragster at Cedar Point in Sandusky, Ohio

Pete Trabucco

the 2006 Golden Ticket awards for the "Best Steel Roller Coaster in the World" category. Riders must be at least fifty-two inches tall to ride.

8 *Volcano—The Blast Coaster* at Paramount's Kings Dominion, Virginia is truly a one-of-a-kind thrill ride contraption! Located in the Congo section of the park, between the *Avalanche Bobsled* coaster and *Outer Limits: Flight of Fear,* the *Volcano* rises above a shady pseudo-tropical landscape that is quite interesting to look at. There truly is nothing like this ride around when it comes to the visuals. Imagine yourself being on an inverted coaster (like *Batman—the Ride*) but instead of going up a lift hill, you are literally launched out of the station, reaching a top speed from zero to seventy mph in less than four seconds. You actually accomplish this without ever climbing a lift hill. Then, while in the middle of this ride, imagine being shot straight up out the top of this volcano to continue your experience, courtesy of a second set of motors.

This type of propulsion system is accomplished using a new concept in motor technology, the Linear Induction Motor system (LI). It is really a very innovative concept that propels a coaster forward on waves of electromagnetic energy. The coaster is blasted quickly to a remarkable velocity, much like being shot out of a cannon, by dozens of these linear induction motors placed around the track. This is what makes this coaster different from your typical gravity (lift hill) coaster. It literally launches the train and its passengers twice, once initially on takeoff, and again after u-turning and heading straight through the top of the volcano. You then streak around the volcano, completing four inversions while flames shoot out from the top of the mountain. On this ride the best place to be is clearly in the *front row,* where the speed and the small clearances around the volcano's exterior make you truly feel like a very fast-moving lava flow.

9 *The Incredible Hulk* at Universal Studio's Islands of Adventure in Orlando, Florida is just a great ride, period! With an angled, dynamic tire-driven launch, riders burst into daylight (or night light) and are immediately flipped upside down. What comes next are seven very quick and enjoyable inversions. Most of this occurs right over the park walkway, and the feeling of speed is clearly felt not just by those who are riding this coaster, but from those watching it on the ground as well. In addition to the tire catapult over water, which they say feels like a cat shot from an aircraft carrier, the immense cobra roll and vertical loop are quite memorable.

Great visuals are also accented in the *Hulk* ride experience. The ride features a mist tunnel and a huge airtime section immediately following the block brake halfway through the ride. This is a section where you think the ride is over, but surprise, surprise. It's not! The ride is incredibly smooth and packs quite a punch throughout for its compact size. If you can experience this coaster at night, where its close proximity to other rides greatly accentuates your view of the park, you will be happy you did. Also, don't forget to enjoy the great queue to start the ride.

One thing to remember about the *Hulk* is that it is best to ride this coaster early. When the park opens, the *Hulk* is the ride you should head to first. If you can take advantage of the park's "Fast Pass" system or stay at one of the local hotels at the park, you surely will be ahead of the waiting game. If not, please note that crowds will generally form for this ride in the late morning and early afternoon, so get there early. You will find the *Hulk* to your left in the superhero section of the park. Or just look up. You won't be able to miss the green track that dangles above you as you enter the land of superheroes. Bolliger and Mabillard really came through with this heroic green monster. Take a ride and see for yourself.

10 *Medusa* at Six Flags Great Adventure in Jackson, New Jersey is also a great ride to experience. Have you ever wanted to be strapped in a chair with your feet dangling precariously while you were fourteen stories high? Better yet, have you ever been strapped to a chair whose sole purpose is to fly through a powerful

Medusa at Six Flags Great Adventure in Jackson, New Jersey

series of twists, turns, and inversions at speeds that reach over sixty mph? If you've answered yes to both questions, then chances are you've experienced the unique, exhilarating, unforgettable thrill from the new generation of man-made adrenaline machines created by Bolliger and Mabillard (B&M) commonly known as the "floorless" roller coasters. *Medusa* went into the history books on April 2, 1999 when it streaked down the tracks as the nation's *first* floorless coaster. This 140-foot monster gives you a great view of the drive-through safari for a brief second before you are dropped at speeds reaching over sixty miles per hour. Since the track is below you and your feet dangle just inches from it, you might want to look anywhere but down at your feet as you speed across the course. Many a rider will try to keep their legs up while traversing the 4000-foot track. This ride is packed with fun, and has seven thrilling inversions guaranteed to put a smile on your face. Inversions include a vertical loop, dive loop, the zero-g roll (the best), Cobra roll (two inversions), and two cork screw turns.

Griffon at Busch Gardens in Williamsburg, Virginia

Pete Trabucco

11 *Griffon* at Busch Gardens in Williamsburg had the biggest and badest dive coaster on the planet. As the name implies, diving coasters climb the lift hill (in this case over 200 feet tall) momentarily hang precariously at the top an then at the time, 90 degrees straight down. To date this is the tallest dive coaster and it sure packs a punch! Griffon evokes the power and speed of a mythical bird that is part eagle and part lion. It plunges, twists and turns - giving riders an adrenaline-pumping adventure that's unlike any coaster experience in the world. As mentioned earlier, Griffon is the tallest dive coaster but at a top speed of 70 miles per hour, it is also the fastest out there. It is also the world's first floorless dive coaster, and the first to incorporate two Immelmann loops, a second 130-foot dive and one water splash down feature. Griffon offers over-the-edge excitement on more than half a mile of steel track and will become the centerpiece of Busch Gardens Europe's French section. The best seat in the house is the front row. Make sure to keep those eyes open when you just hang there for several seconds and take in the view. It is truly worth it. Sure, their might be taller coasters out there but this one will surely make your day and is well worth riding.

12 *Phantoms Revenge* at Kennywood in West Miffin, Pennsylvania is a ride not to be missed. The coaster was originally named The Steel Phantom. It was the first hypercoaster in the world to feature inversions, but this accolade would soon prove to be the downfall of the first version of the coaster. After the 2000 season, *The Steel Phantom* underwent extensive changes by Morgan Manufacturing, most notably the removal of all of its inversions. According to Kennywood, this was done because of many riders' complaints of how rough the coaster was on their heads and necks. This modified coaster reopened for the 2001 season as the *Phantom's Revenge.*

The *Phantom's Revenge* has a top speed of eighty-five mph, putting it in a tie for seventh place of the world's fastest coasters, along with the *Xcelerator* of Knott's Berry Farm. It is currently ranked as the seventh best steel roller coaster in the world according to the editors of *Amusement Today* and is always ranked very high in all major roller coaster surveys. Due to the modifications, both Morgan and Arrow types of track are on the coaster. Although the first hill is only 160 feet high, the second hill drops riders 232 feet into a ravine and through the support structure for *Thunderbolt*. This strategic use of the park's hilly terrain is one of the coaster's most distinguishing features. *Phantom's Revenge* is even bigger and badder than it was with all these inversions. It's not for the faint at heart, this is one of the best rides you will ever get, and views of the Pennsylvania countryside are memorable. The eject action on the bunny hills and the feeling of speed throughout the ride are exceptional. Those that like head chopper action will get that too as they go through the nearby *Thunderbolt* coaster. Roller coaster enthusiasts will agree that the *Phantom* is here to stay and one that will please even the fussiest adrenalin junkie out there.

13 *Superman—Ride of Steel* at Six Flags America, Largo, Maryland, places very high on my list of rides to experience! This ride is, in a word, *fast*. Ranked in the top five in 2004 in the world by *Amusement Park Today,* this coaster created by Interman AG Corporation stands at 209 feet tall and can be clearly seen for miles around the park. It also has one of the steepest first drops (sixty-eight degrees) that there is on such a ride. I will admit, for those who have never ridden mega coasters before, the sight of this contraption can be very daunting, but be assured, looking at it can be quite exciting as well. If you can brave your first reaction to just run away, then all you have to do is strap yourself in and enjoy what follows. Surely you can hide in your seat and take solace in your enclosed car? Wrong! Like its New England and New York sister coasters, the cars have elevated stadium seating and low-slung sides. This was created to better scare the daylights out of you and has gotten many a rider nervous at first. Interman really put in a good effort here with this ride, and until they built the New

Pete Trabucco

Raptor at Cedar Point in Sandusky, Ohio

England version, in my mind *Superman—Ride of Steel* was the best version of its kind.

The difference between this ride and its New England cousin is that, whereas the New England version throws in the best drops and negative-g pullouts you can experience, the Maryland version concentrates on the perception of sheer speed throughout the entire course. The bunny hops at the end are small but very thrilling, and I usually come into the station with a big happy grin on my face. While at this park, try to ride this one last, because after doing *Superman—Ride of Steel* at Six Flags America, all other rides at the park are simply anticlimactic.

14 *Raptor* at Cedar Point in Sandusky, Ohio is one of the best-inverted coasters ever built. *Raptor* rules the sky at Cedar Point! Built in 1994 by the world-renowned team of Bolliger and Mabillard (B & M), Monthey, Switzerland, the *Raptor* roller coaster was voted number eleven in the "Best Steel Roller Coaster in the World" category in a survey conducted by *Amusement Today* in 2005. Guests ride in cars that are suspended from the track above. Specially designed seats allow passengers' legs to dangle, providing the sensation of flight. Aiding that is the fact that riders go upside down six amazing times! The highlight is a first-of-its-kind cobra-roll, a thrilling element that flips riders over, spirals them upside down into a 180-degree roll and repeats the twisting motion in reverse. Looming 137 feet above the main midway and reaching a top speed of fifty-seven mph, *Raptor* is one of the tallest and fastest inverted roller coasters in the world. Nearly 27 million guests have been picked up by the claws of this steel giant since 1994. In 2006, 1,645,189 riders "kicked the sky" on *Raptor*. Guests must be at least fifty-four inches tall to ride.

15 *Superman the Ultimate Flight* at Six Flags, Atlanta, Georgia is like nothing you have ever ridden. *Superman* is only the second B&M coaster in the world where you can literally *fly* around the track. This coaster

Pete Trabucco

Superman the Ultimate Flight at Six Flags, Atlanta, Georgia

offers the rider a sense of flight that can really be intoxicating. On this ride you swoop, dive, and race over the treetops with nothing but an inverted open-air car tethering you. Indeed, it was built upon the idea of taking this coaster to the next level. Flying coasters use an ingenious track layout and a unique coaster car design to replicate the sensation of flight. With special harnesses, there is literally nothing but air separating you and the ground below. It is an odd, but interesting, sensation to hang upside down for what seems to be a long period of time. (The ride itself is only about 140 seconds long.) The inversions on most coasters briefly turn riders upside down, but *Superman* maintains a down position for a large portion of the ride. Packed with five inversions, the ride literally flies you through the course at almost fifty-five miles per hour. Also on the ride, make note that during the top of the pretzel loop, you enter this element on your back and then fly through the loop in a forward position, making it a sensational one-of-a-kind ride experience. You can find another one of these rides at Six Flags Great Adventure in Jackson, New Jersey.

16 *Kumba* at Busch Gardens in Tampa, Florida is quite a coaster and one that was surely created for the masses. At 143 feet high, this was B&M's first traditional sit-down looping coaster, and it has performed that task flawlessly in cars made differently than any other rolling stock. The ride's open airiness and slick design were ahead of their time and one for the record books. In fact, before the notorious *Montu* came into being, this ride was the main reason why coaster enthusiasts came to the park to begin with and is considered one of the main attractions there. Even today, *Kumba* is the largest and fastest coaster you will find in the Southeast. Packed with seven inversions and reaching speeds in excess of sixty mph, this one still holds its own against newer coasters and is well worth the wait that sometimes forms for this ride. It may interest you to know that at one time, *Kumba* was the tallest inverted coaster in the world. In fact, *Kumba* still boasts one of the world's largest vertical loops, reaching a height of 108 feet, and is still considered an intense ride, even by today's standards. The four thousand-foot track seems to wind seamlessly through the beautiful scenery, passing under walkways, through trenches and even over water. Its camelback inversion and cobra roll elements were Bolliger and Mallibard's firsts, and these designs are still used today. *Kumba* blends in with its surroundings, and you really get a feel for the park when ascending that first lift hill. As you know, Busch Gardens is renowned for its animal safaris and nature walks, and from the top of this ride, you can take in the park's beauty (if only for a few seconds) before your inevitable 128-foot plunge down the track to start your greatly accelerated African Adventure. I have heard talk about how rough this ride can be on the human skeletal system. Yes, it may be a little rough by today's standards, but still is pretty smooth as compared to other top coasters I have ridden around the country. I also love the color scheme of aqua blue, yellow, and orange on this ride. It is a colorful way of putting you in the mood for your adventure. A good ride to enjoy with you and your family.

17 *Titan* at Six Flags Over Texas is the fifth tallest coaster (as of this writing) in the nation. *Titan* in my mind is truly a world-class roller coaster and brings to the table some of the best positive-g ride elements ever created for a mega coaster. It is essentially Six Flags Magic Mountain's *Goliath* (255-foot drop, eighty-five mph) with a wicked added upward helix at the block brake. The extra helix makes *Titan* feel like a more complete ride and makes it doubly as intense! It does, however, stand ten feet higher than its west coast counterpart *Goliath* (also created by Giovanola Corporation of Switzerland) and has a pretty steep drop. As you plunge down 255 feet at eighty-five mph into a small tunnel, you will definitely feel you heart pounding.

The drop is good, but what makes this ride experience different from other mega coasters is the *sustained* positive g's that come into play during the second portion of the ride. Usually a rider receives high g-forces for very short time periods. This is not the case with *Titan!* The g-forces on this one can last much longer than on other rides, and they are sustained, so you can experience a brownout or tunnel vision effect similar to that experienced by pilots performing aerobatic maneuvers. I have found that a lot of grunting and groaning helps counteract the effect and keeps the rider more alert and focused on the ride. This is one coaster you have to actually experience in order to enjoy. As a frustrated pilot who loved aerobatics, this one's for me.

At the top of the lift hill, don't forget to look to your left, As an added surprise what you will see is the Ball Park in Arlington where the Major League Texas Rangers play their home games. The ballpark is less than a quarter of a mile away. From where you are sitting, the stadium actually looks dwarfed, making this ride even more impressive! Overall, I found *Titan* to be a pretty intense and enjoyable

Titan at Six Flags Over Texas

Titan at Six Flags Over Texas

ride, but make sure you are ready for those intense positive-g helixes before you attempt this ride.

18 *Dueling Dragons* at Universal Studios Islands of Adventure in Orlando, Florida is a very different and extremely exciting inverted coaster. Your interest in this ride starts as soon as you pass under two menacing statues. One is a fire dragon painted in red and the other is the ice dragon in blue. Once you enter the castle, you experience the best queue area ever designed for a coaster ride. Disney has nothing over this in its repertoire, and you should expect to spend some time just looking at all there is to see in this labyrinth. It is like being in a haunted tomb as you pass frozen or burned knights, depending on which path you take, and learn the story behind these two dragons. When you finally make your choice, please note that each ride is unique, so you want to set aside enough time to ride both while you are there. This is easy to do because after you depart one ride, there is a shortcut to get to the other without having to go in and reenter the castle. B&M has put together a combination of rides that will thrill you, scare you and make you laugh all at the same time.

The rides do all this while consistently maintaining inverted coaster speeds in excess of fifty-five miles per hour while your feet tangle below you. The one element that separates this ride from all others I have ridden is the dual loop, which is timed so that both the fire and ice trains make simultaneous loops during the run. Yes, you heard correctly! Two inverted trains head straight for each other, then at the last moment complete a loop just inches from each other. The ride is timed by computer to make this happen, and it is truly amazing! The best seats for this experience are the front four so you can look directly into the widening eyes of those individuals on the opposite train as they head directly toward you. The closure rate of the two trains is over one hundred mph. Fire and ice are great rides, but make sure you set aside some time to try them both in order for you to get the full riding experience.

19

X2 at Six Flags Magic Mountain in Valencia, California is, in a word, "Revolutionary!" It is truly one of the most highly complex and technically advanced attractions to debut in quite some time. You might not have heard the term "four-dimensional" coaster but after riding *X*, I am here to tell you, that term truly fits this coaster! Created by Arrow Dynamics Corporation in 2002, this incredible ride stands at 190 feet tall and cost over $20 million to build. *X* is a prototype coaster and for the first time ever, riders now sit on the edge of a massive twenty-two-foot wide vehicle that actually spins independently 360 degrees forward and backward during the ride. Plummeting over two hundred feet face first down a near-vertical first drop at seventy-six miles per hour, riders will experience an unprecedented "don't know what to expect" sensation that you just won't find anywhere else. The rotation occurs throughout the ride, so you literally have no idea where you will end up, and if you think you will be able the figure it out, then think again. There is literally nothing else like it

Pete Trabucco

X2 at Six Flags Magic Mountain in Valencia, California

X2 at Six Flags Magic Mountain in Valencia, California

Pete Trabucco

on the planet! *X* is truly different and incomparable to any traditional coaster you have experienced. Honestly, words cannot justly describe the sensation or rush *X* delivers. The secret of *X* can be found in the ride's third rail, which increases and decreases in width, causing the ride vehicle to flip sometimes, depending on the space between the rails. Sounds simple, but I am sure the Arrow experts will disagree with you on that one. Unfortunately with prototypes, this ride (like *Top Thrill Dragster* at Cedar Point) has had some mechanical problems. Having the technology to create a first-of-its-kind ride also means that it takes time to get all the bugs out. This has meant closing the ride and adjusting the ride vehicle at times. But in my mind that is the price you pay for innovation, and in *X* you get just that, with its new and innovative coaster technology. *X* is quite simply a minute of steel mind games over 3610 feet of track that tinkers with your senses, delivering a disorienting experience of fear and joy all at the same time. It is a ride that most everyone will love.

20 *Steel Force* at Dorney Park is one the main reasons why you want to come to this Cedar Fair Park. Ranked sixth in the world in 2002 by *Amusement Today*, this ride really describes what mega coasters are all about. Although very similar to Morgan Manufacturing's other mega coasters, *Mamba* at Missouri Worlds of Fun and *Wild Thing* at Minnesota's Valley Fair, this fast, smooth coaster is near the top of everyone's list. Often compared to *Magnum XL-200* at its sister park in Sandusky Point, Ohio, it measures up and even surpasses *Magnum* in overall thrills. Morgan created an exciting but not too intense ride that drops its riders 205 feet through a long tunnel, along the way managing to give you some unexpected float time on the second hill. After the third hill, the rider is subjected to a descending turnaround helix that shoves you in your seat for some medium g's as you enter the bunny hop section of the ride. Now I don't like to use the word "bunny hop" because it indicates something that this ride definitely does not have. These "hops" range from fifteen to twenty feet high and make you feel like you are literally riding a bucking bronco at the local rodeo. They definitely can't be compared to watching a bunny rabbit scampering around a knoll around Easter time. There is a lot of ejection and float time in this section of the ride that makes it a true gem. When you think you're at the end, the last element sends you through a horizontal double uphill, which you swear is going to send you flying out of your seat. Ride times can vary, but again, try to get to *Steel Force* as early as possible and make this the first ride when you enter the park.

21 *Kraken* at SeaWorld in Orlando, Florida is a very pleasant surprise for all roller coaster enthusiasts tired of the Disney and Universal parks in the area. This ride, along with SeaWorld's water ride "Journey into Atlantis," makes this park a cut above its counterparts around the nation. Created by Bolliger and Mabillard (B&M) and standing at 151 feet high, the ride overlooks the lake and a good portion of the

park. Once on this coaster, the aqua blue, floorless marvel literally sizzles down the track, but watch those feet as you pass the screaming tracks that seem to be just inches from your feet. SeaWorld increased the thrill factor on this ride by straightening out the first drop in order to add more negative g's to the mix. What come next are seven memorable loops at speeds reaching in excess of sixty mph. Three low clearance tunnels highlight the ride, including an unexpected dive and dip through a lagoon. There you will encounter a serpent's underwater lair, complete with live eels. Don't blink or you will surely miss it! Great ride and one worth riding over and over again.

22 *Alpengeist* at Busch Gardens in Williamsburg, Virginia is a lovely, smooth, and graceful inverted coaster. Did I also mention it is the tallest inverted coaster in the world? If you thought *Montu* was all you could handle (once the tallest coaster on the planet), stay away from this monster. *Alpengeist* adds roughly forty-five feet to that former record-holder's 150-foot lift hill. Once you've crested the 195-foot lift hill, a 170-foot drop to the right awaits you and at speeds reaching sixty-seven miles per hour truly gets your blood flowing. *Alpengeist* has a great alpine setting, and from the ski lift design of the cars themselves to the blizzard conditions you notice on the ride, you are about to experience something just a little bit different and unusual. This ride is pretty intense, but since it is much larger than other inverted coasters, I have noticed that you will have a little brake between ride elements.

True, it does have its moments, a ski lift that has gone amok as it races around the six decent inversions. Among these is a distinctive 106-foot high vertical loop, which was one more new record for this inverted coaster. If you can keep your eyes peeled as you streak down the track, you might also spot the poor unfortunate skier who smashed through the top of a house on his way down the hill. You know, the house that you are heading for, directly ahead of you! Also, let's not forget that zero-g roll, the element that B&M have been famous for. They are all here in a coaster that is simply a pure joy to ride! Note: Since all seats have literally closed off any front views, the best visuals occur in the front row only. If you are looking to see it all, you must experience it there. If you want to be surprised, then sit in the back. No matter how you add it up, *Alpengeist* is a destination coaster located at one of the best amusement parks ever created. If you love your coasters, you will cherish this one!

23 *Riddler's Revenge* at Six Flags Magic Mountain in Valencia, California is undoubtedly one of the best stand-up coasters you will find anywhere in the country. Built by Bolliger and Mabillard in 1998, *Riddler's Revenge* is the world's largest stand-up coaster in existence. Themed after *Batman* villain Edward Nygma, also know as "The Riddler," this coaster has continued the Six Flags tradition of designing rides around comic book characters. The adventure begins as guests are drawn into the attraction by a glowing green neon entrance which is disguised as a question mark. Once inside, guests witness mysterious and chaotic experiments of mind-bending proportions in the confines of the Riddler's laboratory prior to boarding. After boarding the Riddler's latest creation of sleek green trains, riders are carried up the 156-foot tall lift hill. Within seconds of reaching the top, the train makes a quick 180-degree turn and then dives 146 feet into a vertical loop, the first of six inversions. The *Riddler* continues to twist the rider's mind with two consecutive dive loops, followed by an inclined loop, while traveling at speeds of up to sixty-five mph. As the train accelerates, riders travel through a barrel roll over a bunny hop and into a gravity-defying upward spiral. But wait, it's not over, there remains one more brain-tossing barrel roll left in its 4370-foot track. As the train finally returns to the laboratory, some three minutes later, you will find that this is an ultra smooth stand-up ride (unlike some other stand-ups I have ridden— Ouch!) that the coaster enthusiast will love. If you're not crazy about stand-up coasters, this one could be the one that changes your mind about them. It just also happens to be the biggest and best of them all!

24 *Hypersonic XLC* at Paramount's Kings Dominion is the closest that you'll ever come to the feeling of being shot off a Naval Aircraft Carrier (that is, before the latest rocket coaster came into existence). Without a doubt the experience is for some *incredible* and for others, *quite painful!* You can actually feel your face start to fold as you accelerate from 0 to 80 mph in less than two seconds. After liftoff, the rider experiences a hill (straight up) of 165 feet, followed by a drop, straight down for the most part, of 133 feet. Not bad for those who like to ride on the wild side. The only problem here is that after these two amazing elements, there is nothing left but a high-speed turn-around section and one small hill as you head back to the station. Some other LSM and LIM coasters match or even exceed *Hypersonic's* top speed, but as stated earlier, none of them achieve these speeds as quickly as this one, zero to eighty mph in one point eight seconds, unless you include the king of this type of ride, *Top Thrill Dragster* located at Cedar Point, or *Kingda Ka* at Six Flags Great Adventure. It should, however, be noted that *Hypersonic* came first. Because the coaster uses pneumatic tires and a unique shock absorption system, it's a ride that is also amazingly smooth. Add to the speed and slick track a death-defying vertical hill, and you have a pretty good ride combination. The concept is great, and S & S Power Corporation (of drop/lift tower fame) should be commended for this innovative first attempt. I have heard that newer, taller, and longer versions of this ride from S & S are popping up around the world, and that is great, since this concept of high speed, comfortable trains and straight up/down drops is quite exciting to any coaster enthusiast. Like all e-ticket rides, you might want to get to *Hypersonic* early in the day. Since only one train of eight riders can go at any given time, the lines can be quite long.

25 *Great Bear* at Hershey Park in Pennsylvania is an excellent ride and one that when built in 1998 had taken the inverted coaster concept to the next level. Most B&M inverted coasters seem to have similar pacing, but this one clearly breaks that mold. *Great Bear* starts out differently in that instead of plunging from a height of 124 feet straight down to start the ride, it actually helixes into a double dip before the expected plummet. That's when you know this ride is going to be a far different experience. The inversions over the pond are splendid and overall the four inversions you encounter along the way are pretty intense. One of these inversions actually goes through one of the supports of the ride, giving the rider an "eye of the needle" effect. *Great Bear* also finds itself (and you) wrapped around one of the first looping coasters ever built, *Superdooperlooper,* which makes for an amazing photo opportunity for your friends watching as you race through this section of track. Except for one dead spot toward the end of the ride, *Great Bear* can definitely be rated high as one that everyone can enjoy. The lines for this ride can get long, however, so I suggest you ride this one early.

26 *Batman the Dark Knight* at Six Flags New England might appear to be a short ride, but in my mind, it is one of the most intense floorless coasters I have experienced! Standing at 117 feet high, this Bolliger and Mabillard concoction debuted in April of 2002. It might not be the tallest floorless coaster around, but it doesn't need to be. Like the original *Batman— the Ride*, counterpart *Dark Knight* maintains a small footprint in its 2600 feet of track, and like *Batman* travels at sustained top speeds of fifty-five miles per hour. This makes all turns sharp and the g-forces high during a good portion of the ride. Inversions include a dive loop, vertical loop, a sweet zero-g roll and two interlocking flat spins. Unlike traditional roller coasters, *Batman the Dark Knight* utilizes floorless trains. Once the passenger is strapped into the pedestal-style seats, the floor drops away, providing the floorless effect we all have heard about. What this means is that the rider gets to sit in an open "flying chair" and watch the track below speeding just inches under their legs. This is a unique floorless coaster to ride, and even though it is quite short (not quite two and a half minutes long) it can get quite intense. On floorless coasters all seats are pretty good, but I prefer the back row on this ride. The purple and black paint scheme is a mood setter for this innovative coaster which is guaranteed to be a crowd pleaser, especially for those who would like to experience the next level of coaster enthusiasm.

27 *Batwing* at Six Flags America is a really interesting and innovative ride. I was in Washington on business and heard the hype about these new flying coasters, so I thought I would see what all the excitement was about. *Batwing* is only the second coaster in the world where you can literally *fly* around the track. This coaster offers the rider a sense of flight that can really be described as intoxicating. On *Batwing,* you swoop, dive, and race over the treetops with nothing but an inverted open-air car tethering you. Indeed Vekoma has built upon their reputation by taking this coaster to the next level. Flying coasters, like

Six Flags America's *Batwing,* use an ingenious track layout and a unique coaster car design to replicate the sensation of flight. With special harnesses made for the occupant, there is literally nothing but air separating you and the ground below. It is an odd, but interesting, sensation to hang upside down for what seems to be a long period of time. (The ride itself is only about 140 seconds long.) The inversions on most coasters briefly turn riders upside down, but *Batwing* maintains a down position for a large portion of the ride. At first, the urge is to hang on for dear life. (I know I did that.) However, as the ride progresses, you realize that you can trust the harnesses, stretch out your arms and fly like Superman through the corkscrews and additional elements on this ride. At 3340 feet long and 115 feet high, *Batwing* delivers some sensational stuff for the roller coaster enthusiast who likes to try new things. Packed with five inversions, you literally find yourself flying through the course at almost fifty miles per hour. Also on the ride, make note that during the loop, the rider enters on their back and then flies through the loop in a forward position, making *Batwing* a sensational one-of-a-kind ride experience. In addition to *Batwing,* there are currently three "flying Dutchman" coasters in existence. One is *Stealth* at Six Flags Great America, and the other is *X Flight* at Six Flags World of Adventure.

28 *Expedition Everest* located at Disney's Animal Kingdom in Orlando is one fantastic ride experience. As you walk past to mountain and get a glimpse of one of the rides drops and turnaround, you can see that any resemblance to the Matterhorn in Disneyland is practically non existent. Sure you are entering a mountain, and yes you will see a fierce yeti inside the structure but from that point on the ride is absolutely different and very memorable. Riders will be quickly shocked to see that a piece of switch tracks flip over so that these same riders will have to retrace their route through the mountain and they must do this in the dark and going *backward*...The coaster hurtles backward into the mountain's dark void. The track banks and the positive G-forces push the lap bars into riders and the riders into their seats. It's a strange and disorienting sensation to be blindly racing backward and to feel the strong gravitational pull. Riders' thrill tolerances and coaster savvy will help determine the ratio of giddiness to dread they will experience. The train screeches to a halt again, this time on a decline, and a projected shadow image of the yeti is seen ripping up another section of the track. The train proceeds forward, plunges down the front of the mountain (smile, this is where your photo is snapped), and with the destroyed track, sends riders freefalling to their apparent doom. Instead, the coaster careens in and out of the mountain for some high-speed, banked-curve action. Before returning to the station, the coaster makes one last pass through the mountain, and the enormous yeti takes a convincing swipe at riders with his oversized paw. With the coaster flying past, the encounter lasts a mere second or two, but the effect is wild. The yeti is Disney's most sophisticated animatronics figure to date, and be advised that it will definitely scare younger passengers.

When Animal Kingdom opened, it was criticized that the park had very few attractions worth experiencing. Expedition Everest, which reportedly cost $100 million, marks the first Animal Kingdom ride to acknowledge the fact that park goers are looking for a little more thrill and with this ride addition, has succeeded in putting this park on par with all other Disney parks in the Orlando area.

29 *Rock-n-Roller Coaster* at Disney's MGM Studios in Florida takes you through southern California on what can best be described as a real long *limo*. The *Rock-n-Roller Coaster* rocks and rolls at the end of the park's Sunset Boulevard and is situated right next to The Twilight Zone's *Tower of Terror*. Created by Vekoma Corporation, this ride shoots you (LSM style) out of the gate doing zero to fifty mph in less than three seconds. It then carries you through three inversions on your way to an *Aerosmith* concert that, of course, you are really late for. Your only warning to the start of the ride is *Aerosmith* lead singer Steven Tyler saying, "Are you ready *to rock?* Then let's get it *on!*" At that point the light turns green and you are catapulted out of the station, up a double-inverting rollover loop (B & M Cobra roll) twisting and turning, flipping and rising, falling and charging through the dark of a simulated night sky (all in relative darkness). After this eye-opening element, you peel around banked curves, flying past palm trees, Randy's Donuts, interstate freeway markers, and through the "O" of the famous Hollywood sign. You are literally traffic jammin' with pedal to the metal all the way to the concert. Finally, you set up for the last inversion, a corkscrew maneuver that seems much smaller and tighter than this same element anywhere else. Vekoma takes this ride to the next level by blasting out music as you fly down the track. That's right; while on your trip you will hear five synchronized audio scores from *Aerosmith* blasting out of nine hundred speakers built throughout the *limo.* You never wanted to be a rock star more in your life than

on this ride! At least you can feel like one anyway. Overall, it's a real fun experience and you will also love the twenty-minute pre-show that only Disney magic can create. This pre-show and the queue really do set the mood for your memorable ride. Since Walt Disney World theme parks have "Fast Pass," there really aren't any extremely long lines, but plan on experiencing this ride early in the morning as soon as you enter the park, right before or after Disney's other main attraction, *Tower of Terror.*

30 *Maverick* at Cedar Point in Sandusky, Ohio. Get ready to experience the best new ride out there. This one will make you realize that imagination is all you need to succeed. Maverick, Cedar Point's 17th amazing roller coaster first introduced in 2007 was voted the Best New Ride of 2007 by *Amusement Today's* panel of experts in the newspaper's annual Golden Ticket Awards but is still a top pick today. Located in Frontiertown, this $21 million marvel is a coaster unlike any other at the park and does something that very few coasters can boast.

Maverick at Cedar Point in Sandusky, Ohio

Pete Trabucco

It not only drops straight down but at 95 degrees, you are actually heading past that mark. Guests begin their adventurous journey on Maverick by boarding steam-era-styled, coaster trains with an ultra-sleek profile that carry them along the 4,450-foot-long course. Linear motors propel the train to the top of a 105-foot-tall first hill. From there, as explained earlier, it's not straight down! Maverick takes its passengers down to past the 90-degree angle at speeds of up to 57 mph. Only at about 5 feet from the ground do you pull out of this hair-raising dive. From there, the train hugs the terrain as it twists and banks around hairpin turns with quick but smooth changes in direction. Throughout the 2-minute, 30-second ride, passengers also experience eight "airtime-filled hills," two inversions and a second launch through a dark tunnel that leaves riders wanting for more as you race across the 4,450 foot track at speeds of 70 mph. With an initial drop a mere 100-feet, it looks like you are about to ride a coaster in the family coaster class. Especially when right next-door you have the 300 and 400-foot profiles of the park's Millennium Force

and Top Thrill Dragster. However, stats and looks can be deceiving and this is so true when talking about this ride. This bucking bronco got the goods and even though it never lets up, the ride is smooth and quick. The seating of ten riders across is also a first for the industry and for the best seat, the front row is the ticket. Don't pass this one up if you are in this park.

Bonus Steel Coasters:

There are so many great coasters, I had to mention these as well. They might not have made the top 30 but they are well worth mentioning.

Flight of Fear at Paramount's Kings Dominion is comparable to Disney's *Space Mountain* on steroids. With a four and a half g liftoff into a dark and strange world, you might compare this ride to *Rock-n-Roller Coaster* (Disney MGM) in its overall presentation. The difference here is that this particular ride made the history books as the first LIM/LSM catapult ride when it debuted in June of 1996. You will also find that this is the same premier ride you find at other parks (like *Joker's Jinx* at SFA), but unlike the others, this one is set in the dark for overall effect. *Flight of Fear* may be old, but coaster enthusiasts will find it to be in great shape for its age! I found it to be a good ride, and with the new lap bar setup (replacing the old horse-collar configuration), it was much more comfortable on the head and neck area. The best seats on this ride are clearly the front two. I also have found that there really isn't much of a wait for this ride, even though Kings Dominion offers many heavy-hitter thrill rides. What this means to you is that you can ride this attraction many times during the day with literally no wait. Recommended for coaster enthusiasts who want to try something a bit different, and as a warm-up to the all the e-ticket rides at this park. You will truly enjoy yourself here.

Montezooma's Revenge at Knott's Berry Farm in California is a classic ride for just about everyone. It is one of the last Schwarzkopf shuttle loop coasters to operate in the US, and at just eight hundred feet long

maintains one of the smallest footprints in the park. Small imprint, yes, but long on intensity for a ride that was built before most coaster enthusiasts were even born. The coaster train is launched out of the station, attaining speeds of just over fifty-five miles per hour in only four and a half seconds. It then races up a loop, down the other side, and to the top of the 70-degree incline spike on the opposite side, where it reaches a height of around 150 feet. There it loses its inertia and freefalls backward through the loop toward and through the station and back up another spike (angled at seventy degrees), finally dropping back toward the station and stopping on a dime. It is amazing to be sitting, stopping, and then dropping at a seventy-degree angle in that last element while the ground is quickly rushing toward you. All through this experience the train is also equipped with only a single lap bar holding you in, allowing for maximum enjoyment. Back in 1978 this coaster was it! Today the ride is still a contender in my books.

There are two variations of the catapult system: weight drop and flywheel. The weight drop uses a forty-ton weight in a tower at the end of the ride.

Pete Trabucco

The weight connects to a pulley system, which triples the speed of the drop, placing over thirteen tons of force on the train. The flywheel utilizes a six-ton flywheel in a machine room in front of the loop. The flywheel spins to 1044 rpm and then engages a four to one ratio speed reducer. This turns a drive pulley and propels the train via a cable system. *Montezooma* uses the flywheel method to propel its riders down the track and makes the ride much quicker than its predecessor's system. The flywheel launch, although not as impressive as today's LIM/LSM launches, still gets your attention because this launch technique is much louder on the ears than a standard LIM/LSM launch. The return trip of this marvel back through the station and up the opposite spike is almost deafening for those waiting to ride. The presence of *Jaguar*'s track (another coaster at the park) within the loop adds to the pucker factor for the coaster enthusiast. Those who want to move to a more advanced level of coasters should try this one. It is definitely a pleasant surprise in a very nice and interesting park.

Big Bad Wolf at Busch Gardens in Williamsburg is arguably the best of the Arrow suspended roller coasters running today. There are a few suspended coasters out there, but this one truly surpasses them all. Do not confuse a suspended roller coaster with an inverted coaster such as *Batman—the Ride*. Originally Arrow's suspended coasters were created to complete inversion elements (loops, corkscrews, etc.). Unfortunately the ride's vehicles' swing capability and the actual weight of the cars themselves made it a technical nightmare to achieve. If the train wasn't traveling fast enough when it went through a particular inversion, the cars would fall to the side fast, and well, you can imagine what might then happen to its passengers. That would not have been good for this park nor for the amusement park industry. But the swaying action actually made this coaster a bit more interesting to many a coaster fan. It is a general opinion for all those who ride this classic that no inversions are really needed. The combined fast track, beautiful settings, and crazy cars that seem to have a mind of their own make this one great ride from beginning to end. This ride features two distinct phases:

the first is a series of very tight swings (and I mean tight) through a Bavarian Village, followed by a second chain lift (one hundred feet) and an eye-opening second drop down to the park's Rhine River. Created in 1984, the original footers and overall layout are said to have been created by Anton Schwarzkopf himself. Traveling around the park at speeds of almost fifty miles per hour, what makes this ride different are those swaying trains. I have seen coaster enthusiasts who have ridden the huge mega coasters strap into this ride and be amazed (and sometimes scared) at this ride experience. But you can relax, my daughter went on this ride at age seven and loved every minute of it. The *Big Bad Wolf* is a great ride at any time of the day, but I like to ride it at night or just after a nice rainfall. The track is slicker at this time and more movement can be felt in the trains.

Shockwave at Six Flags over Texas is a wonderful Anton Schwarzkopf design that all roller coaster buffs will enjoy. Created in 1976 and standing at 116 feet high, *Shockwave* reaches speeds of sixty miles per hour and is one of the largest steel coasters of this type. *Shockwave* combines powerful positive g's in its back-to-back seventy-foot loops, while also giving the rider surprisingly strong negative-g drops. And unlike other compact portable coasters of this genre, at 3600 feet long, this coaster covers a lot of ground. Enjoyed by many, this ride is a classic and still highly ranked in all coaster polls I have seen. Also, on *Shockwave*, there are no horse-collar restraints to get in the way. On this ride, you only have a lap bar between you and the ground, and that, my friends, makes all the difference. When at Six Flags over Texas, make this coaster one of your first stops (after *Titan* and *Texas Giant*), as lines can get quite long at this Six Flags park.

The Laser at Dorney Park in Pennsylvania is truly a pleasant surprise. We know why we head to this park, to be tested by *Steel Force* or maybe *Talon*, but while you are here, you can still enjoy the simple pleasure of *The Laser*. Like *Shockwave* in Texas, this is a standard double loop twister built by the Anton Schwarzkopf in 1986. Standing at only ninety-three feet tall, it offers a truly intense ride for its size. There are very strong positive g's

Pete Trabucco

through the loop, like all Schwarzkopf inventions, and the turns are rather smooth. The rolling stock cars, aside from tracking well, afford a very open view and feature only ratcheting lap bars to hold you in your seat. On *Laser* you receive two minutes of coaster pleasure racing around the course at around fifty miles per hour. This is a good intermediate coaster for the budding roller coaster enthusiast. Unfortunately there is one downer to this ride: you can't pick your seat. Riders enter the station and are assigned seats as they enter, so you never know where you are going to end up. Even though this is not the reason why you come to Dorney Park, it is a good coaster to go to when the lines are too long at the e-ticket rides.

Joker's Jinx at Six Flags America is a great ride for those who like something a little bit different. At the time of this writing there were only four of these premier-built LIM spaghetti track rides in North America. (Two were put indoors, *Flight of Fear* at Paramount's Kings Dominion and Kings Island theme parks, and *Poltergeist* at Six Flags Fiesta Texas.) When you enter this ride, you will notice that its queue is second to none. Everything is painted in neon lime green, pink, yellow, and purple colors when you enter this warehouse, which has been converted into a fun house, and see the colorful trains ready to take you on your fast trip. At this point you can't help but wonder how you are going to navigate the spaghetti-type track that you see before you. With a zero to sixty mph in three seconds, linear induction motor sendoff, and purple columns flying very closely by your head, the next four inversions are quite fun. All you can see at times is a lot of twisting and turning metal as you navigate the course, but I assure you, it's fun to experience being a very large mouse in an even larger maze. I noticed only one dead spot on this ride, where the car slows down just so the rider can really get a handle on his bearings. *Joker's Jinx*, originally equipped with horse-collar (over the shoulder) harnesses, became a much more comfortable and exciting ride when the harnesses were replaced with a simple hugging lap bar arrangement. The technology (linear induction process) created here was a first of its kind, and I am told that even NASA had an interest in this ride when it first opened in 1999. Overall you will have a good ride experience on *Joker's Jinx*. It will not feel too intense, but it in no way can be compared to any family coaster you have ridden. It simply is a fun coaster to ride, and I highly recommend it!

Loch Ness Monster at Busch Gardens Williamsburg, Virginia, often called *Nessie* like its namesake, is one of the most unique designs ever created by the Arrow Corporation. Looking over the edge of this coaster, 130 feet high, you can really appreciate its beauty as you plummet 115 feet down the fifty-five-degree first drop into the interlocking loops of this classic coaster. The interlocking loops look much more imposing than they actually are, but they are the main reason you want to ride this puppy. Created in 1978 and the first of its kind, this coaster streaks along the 3240-foot track at speeds of up to sixty miles per hour. Although not as intense as other rides in the park, the *Loch Ness Monster* features tunnels, two lift hills and great use of the local terrain to give you one great ride! The only thing I was not impressed with was the horse-collar harness. They are

quite old and seem not to fit very well on the car itself. They will need to be replaced sometime in the future. On busy days the ride is timed so that both trains enter the interlocking loops at the same time, making for a real unique experience. The best seats for visuals on this ride are the front two seats, but if you really want to get a real unbelievable ride, then the back car is for you. After my experience in the back, I was more than ready to make that appointment with my local chiropractor!

Great American Scream Machine at Six Flags Great Adventure in Jackson, New Jersey was a big deal when it first opened in 1989. Created by Arrow Dynamics, this coaster was the second of Six Flags' record-breaking trio of looping coasters. The first was *Shockwave* at Six Flags Great America in Illinois, and the third was *Viper* at Six Flags Magic Mountain in California. All three stand at over 170 feet tall and speed around the track at sixty-eight miles per hour. The *Scream Machine* is the tallest of the three (at 173 feet) and has a 155-foot twisting drop to the left before undergoing seven memorable inversions. The first loop stands at 136 feet tall, a record at one time, and

Loch Ness Monster at Busch Gardens Williamsburg, Virginia

America's Top Roller Coasters & Amusement Parks

sets up the rider for a slew of loops that will definitely disorient you. I must admit, the one real drawback of this ride is that the old horse-collar restraints might be a little uncomfortable when you compare them to today's new harnesses. Still, like its sister coasters, it is a good ride. I really enjoy riding this coaster at night, when you really get a great view of the park. Since the lift hill takes you directly over the park itself, you get a great view of the entire Great Adventure layout and can compare your overall height (second tallest coaster at Six Flags Great Adventure; *Nitro* is number one at 230 feet) to other award-winning coasters in the park. This is a great coaster for the enthusiast who wants to move up to the next level of intense roller coaster rides, but watch out. It can be a real head-banger at times.

Batman and Robin—The Chiller at Six Flags Great Adventure in Jackson, New Jersey was truly one of a kind, even though you will see similar rides all around the country! *One coaster* that I will surely miss will be this one…No longer with us but ever present in my memory was *Batman and Robin—The Chiller* was torn down in the spring of 2008 to make room for the family coaster "The Dark Knight." Following the success of the first ride to apply the linear induction technology with *Flight of Fear*, Six Flags asked Premier to create for them a new and unusual LIM-launched ride. Premier came back with not one but two rides for the Six Flags Corporation. They created *Batman and Robin—the Chiller;* a ride that has two very different elements and track lengths, and you get to choose which experience you want to experience. When you go through the queue area, you get to pick the ride you want (Batman or Robin). The choice is simple and the line becomes the bigger problem of the day. When you are in the launch bay area, you are strapped into fairly comfortable seats and wait for the countdown to occur. "Three, two, one-Launch!" What you will then feel is an incredible rush of air that catapults you from zero to seventy mph in just four seconds on a spectacular linear induction motor-launched coaster created by Force Engineering.

Each track of this dual coaster is similar but does have certain differences that enhance your ride experiences. While riding Batman, the blue track where the train launches you through a tunnel, straight up ninety degrees into a "top hat" inversion (a half loop), straight down ninety degrees, into a heart line corkscrew, and through another LIM launch as you roll to the top of the two hundred-foot dead end. At this point you start to fall down, dropping backward through another LIM system and back through the ride elements described above.

On Robin (the red track), the track is essentially the same *except* that instead of the ninety degree up/tophat/ninety degree down section, an incredibly fast two-inversion cobra roll maneuver is achieved, followed by the same heart line corkscrew element. The Robin track is a bit longer (because of the boomerang roll) at 1229 feet as opposed to Batman's 1137 total track length. Both rides are truly fun to experience. Also, this ride has improved drastically since the horse-collar restraint system was removed in favor of a state of the art lap bar arrangement. Far less head banging occurs with this upgrade. *The Chiller* in the past has had several problems in the maintenance department, and you will rarely find that both sides are operating at the same time.

Because of this, it is advisable to make this one a top priority (after *Nitro* of course) and get in line early in the morning.

The Chiller had been known to keep you waiting as long as ninety minutes for your rendezvous with destiny. The Chiller will surely be missed!

America's 30 Best
Wooden Roller Coasters

1. *The Voyage* at Holiday World, Santa Claus, Indiana.

2. *Thunderhead* at Dollywood in Pigeon Forge, Tennessee

3. *Boulder Dash* at Lake Compounce in Bristol, Connecticut.

4. *The Raven* at Holiday World, Santa Claus, Indiana.

5. *Ghostrider* at Knott's Berry Farm in Buena Park, California.

6. *El Toro* at Six Flags Great Adventure, Jackson, New Jersey.

7. *The Phoenix* at Knobels in Elysburg, Pennsylvania.

8. *Shivering Timbers* at Michigan Adventures in Muskegon, Michigan.

9. *The Beast* at Paramount's Kings Island in Kings Mills, Ohio.

10. *The Texas Giant* at Six Flags over Texas.

11. *Lightning Racer* at Hershey Park in Pennsylvania.

12. *The Cyclone* at Astroland Park in Coney Island, New York.

13. *Rampage* at Visionland in Bessemer, Alabama.

14. *The Comet* at Six Flags Great Escape Fun Park, Lake George, NY.

15. *Twister* at Knobles in Elysburg, Pennsylvania.

16. *Gwazi* at Busch Gardens in Tampa, Florida.

17. *Great White* at Morey's Pier in Wildwood, New Jersey.

18. *Giant Dipper* at Belmont Park in San Diego, California.

19. *The Wild One* at Six Flags America, Largo, Maryland.

20. *Roar* at Six Flags America, Largo, Maryland.

21. *Puma Roller Coaster* at Clementon Park, Clementon, New Jersey.

22. *The Wildcat* at Hershey Park in Hershey, Pennsylvania.

23. *The Riverside Cyclone* at Six Flags New England, Agawam, Massachusetts.

24. *Rebel Yell* at Paramount's Kings Dominion, Virginia.

25. *Thunderhawk* at Dorney Park in Allentown, Pennsylvania.

26. *Thunderbolt* at Six Flags New England.

27. *The Comet* at Hershey Park, Hershey, Pennsylvania.

28. *Rolling Thunder* at Six Flags Great Adventure, Jackson, New Jersey.

29. *The Dragon Coaster* at Playland Park, Rye, New York.

30. *The Jack Rabbit* at Clementon Park, Clementon, New Jersey (SBNO)

1 *The Voyage* at Holiday World, Santa Claus, Indiana is a hybrid wooden roller coaster, which opened in May 2006 at Holiday World, an amusement park located in Santa Claus, Indiana. A wooden hybrid consists of a steel structure with wood track. The Voyage has a lift hill of 163 feet, followed by drops of 154 feet, 107 feet and 100 feet. It travels underground through tunnels eight times. It is the third longest wooden coaster in the world at 6,442 feet and fourth fastest at 67.4 mph. In addition, *The Voyage* has the most air time of any wooden roller coaster in the world with 24.2 seconds and features three 90-degree banked turns. The Voyage is also the sixth tallest wooden roller coaster. In 2006, The Voyage won the Best New Ride Award at the

Golden Ticket. In 2007, The Voyage was awarded the title of Best Wooden Coaster at the same ceremony. Right now ranked as the best wooden coaster by *Amusement Today*. This ride has set the mark for all wooded coasters to beat. It's a ride and a half and one of my favorite coasters on this list.

2 *Thunderhead* at Dollywood at Pigeon Forge, Tennessee is a ride that you will find has few peers in the thrill ride circuit. One of the main features of the ride you will notice is how twisted the layout is. Just in the first thirty seconds of the ride, you will cross over and under the track (eight) times. There are over thirty cross-overs and -unders making the *Thunderhead* the most twisted ride so far. We dare you to come off the ride and draw out the layout without looking at the ride. It's impossible to get it right the first time! *Thunderhead* is Great Coasters International's tallest coaster so far with a one hundred-foot lift hill and many unique features like seventy-eight degree banked turns and the first ever station fly-through element. These turns are very similar to another great coaster by the name of *Millennium Force* and fall short of their bank by just two degrees.

Once the train crests the lift hill, the thrill begins early with an insane twisted first drop. The best seat on this ride is the back with all the twists and turns that set up for this ride. The airtime received will be that similar to the *Legend* coaster that is also listed as one of my top coasters in this book. After a turnaround similar to *Millennium,* what lies ahead is an element that you will find interesting and what sets this ride apart for all the others. It's called the station fly-through. When you get close to the station, it looks as if you are going to hit the roof. If you are waiting at the station, the sound of the coaster above will surely wake you up as it flies above at forty miles per hour. *Thunderhead* lives up to its name and when you leave the station, you will surely feel like you been through a storm of immense proportion. A ride that surely needs to be experienced first hand...

3 *Boulder Dash* at Lake Compounce in Bristol, Connecticut, is in my mind one of the very best, wooden coasters ever created. Upon boarding one of the two spacious Philadelphia Toboggan Company trains, your journey begins with a serene and picturesque trip up the lift hill. Cresting into a scenic ninety-degree turn, riders are given just enough time to relax before the drop and a ride you will not soon forget! This coaster has it all. At 4500 feet long, *Boulder Dash* is to date the *only* coaster that literally was built along the side of a mountain. It is one of the largest and fastest wood coasters I have ridden to date. At 155 feet high and reaching speeds of sixty mph, all the pieces come together in a presentation that constantly gives you a fun-filled thrill ride experience. It is a smooth and great family coaster, set up in one of the most family-oriented amusement parks I have been to. I consistently get off this ride feeling like I really got my money's worth. The trick I think is that since most of the course is wooded, you never do know what's up ahead. The ride literally dashes through trees and around rocks,

and unlike most wooden coasters has a consistent ride throughout. The majestic mountain setting also makes this ride a one-of-a-kind experience. Ranked by *Amusement Today* as one of the top five best coasters on the planet (and after riding it, I can see why), there really isn't a bad seat anywhere. I have ridden on most of them! However, I will tell you that I prefer the front row on this one. A great ride for everyone this is a coaster well worth waiting in line for, and the best news is that there are very rarely long lines at this top attraction.

4 *The Raven* at Holiday World opened in 1995 to rave reviews by most coaster enthusiasts. GCI (Great Coasters International) put together a gem when they laid out the course for the *Raven*. The thing I really like about the *Raven* is the sustained speed and relentless power around its 2800-foot track, something that very few coasters around the country have been successfully able to achieve. The *Raven* is indeed a world-class coaster which features a lot of speed, airtime, lateral forces, and both positive and negative g's throughout the ride. During the course, the ride makes a u-turn to the lift hill and is unusually fast then a right turn to the first drop which features good airtime in both the back and the middle of the train. The bottom of the eighty-six-foot drop has a tunnel (which is really enjoyable), followed by a small drop and a larger nice third drop.

Immediately following this drop is what I feel is the nicest part of the ride. The train takes you over what I call the "lake turn," which is extremely fast and contains pretty good lateral forces. Another small drop then occurs, taking the train slightly upward toward an awesome fifth drop with extreme airtime for all seats. The second part of the course is comprised of hairpin turns, multiple direction changes, and small hops which take your breath away. The *Raven* is by far one of the best-designed and powerful wooden coasters that I have ridden, with a well-hidden layout and multiple surprises along the way. *The Raven* is easily the best terrain woodie in the world and holds its own amongst the biggest and

the best. A night ride on the *Raven* is coaster riding at its very best, an experience to be savored by any coaster enthusiast. The darkness, wind, airtime, stars, and wonderful train and track noise only a wooden coaster can produce add up to a magical experience. I would recommend this woodie any day of the week.

5 *Ghostrider* at Knott's Berry Farm in Buena Park, California is an extremely fast and exciting twister that fits beautifully in the western theme of the park. The Ghost Town section of the park is a fitting place for this coaster to be. I like the attraction's queue. After a couple of twists and turns through the mine shaft, you emerge onto a woodsy path that takes you past the coaster's first maneuver, a dipping spiral that drops out of the station and turns the train around toward the base of the lift hill. It sets you up for what is surely going to be a great ride. As you ascend the lift hill, there are a few moments left for you to twist around and check out the view of some of Knott's vertical icons: the *Parachute Drop,* the *Supreme Scream* tower, and

Voyage at Holiday World

Timber Mountain. On the left side you can see the *Ghostrider's* L-shaped, double-layered, out and back path. At 118 feet high, *Ghostrider* features a steep 110-foot drop and races around the course at over fifty-five miles per hour. On this ride you definitely get that "out of control" feeling as you continually go back into its structure, and it constantly gives you that head-chopper effect that is so prevalent in this type of coaster.

Since this ride is located in an earthquake zone, additional wood was needed in order to fit California state guidelines. This makes for an impressive super-structure that can't be seen, so the rider has no idea where you are going. At 4500-feet long, you are just turning around when most coasters are heading into the station. This ride was recently rated second in the top ten rides on a recent A & E poll, and after riding it countless times, I can see why. The top ride in that poll was *Millennium Force* in Sandusky, Ohio, putting *Ghostrider* in good company. This ride is fast, and when you combine speed with the extreme airtime you

Pete Trabucco

experience on every hill, you can see why it is so popular with coaster enthusiasts around the world.

6 *El Toro* at Six Flags Great Adventure in Jackson, New Jersey is one of the best wooden roller coasters on the Northeast! Riding *El Toro* is something any coaster enthusiast, should put on their list of coasters to conquer. With one of the steepest drops (seventy-six degrees) on the planet and the feeling of full speed ahead throughout the ride, *El Toro* is unmatched for its tenacity and reridability. The fast lift hill reminiscent of *Millennium Force* keeps you guessing on what will be next. The placement of this ride is also something to marvel at. The *El Carnival* section is appropriately themed with a Spanish flare. Situated where the *Old Viper* coaster was, the ride fits perfectly into the area perfectly and delivers more thrills than most other Six Flags rides combined at the park. The trains are themed somewhat like mine train cars and have a very comfortable, next generation look and feel. Loading the trains is a bit slow, but the trains

El Toro at Six Flags Great Adventure in Jackson, New Jersey

are longer than normal holding thirty-six riders compared to twenty-four on *Thunderhead* and the twenty-eight stowed on *The Voyage*. The height of *El Toro* (176 feet) may not be the tallest around but that first drop is a memorable one, and I have to say one of the best first drops that I have experienced on a wooden coaster. The overall out and back (with a twist) coaster reminded me a lot of *Shivering Timbers* at Michigan Adventure but with a lot more pop in the saddle. What I found most interesting even though this is a very intense ride, was how smooth it was throughout. You would think you were riding a steel coaster (like *Nitro*) but you are on wood. The airtime of *El Toro* is sensational and *Intamin's Prefabricated Wooden Coaster* in my mind really delivers a real bang for the buck. This is the type of coaster you seek out, and along with *Nitro* and *Kingda Ka* are the sole reasons why you come to this Six Flags park.

7 *The Phoenix* at Knobels in Elysburg, Pennsylvania is one great classic coaster! Its double out and back design is one of the best there is. Built in 1940 by PTC/Herb Schmeck and named *Rocket* when it resided at Playland Park in San Antonio, Texas, it was relocated to its present site in 1985. Coaster designer Charles Dinn, who created the *Beast,* was asked to reconstruct this gem of a ride in the Pennsylvania mountains and he succeeded marvelously. *Phoenix* is the coaster lover's perfect combination of a classic out and back with some unique elements. First there is an amazingly long (and might I add very dark) tunnel which succeeds in significantly disorienting your perception of what lay ahead. All of a sudden you emerge behind the station and begin the seventy-eight-foot climb up that famous lift topped with a stylish cupola. After a steep seventy-two-foot first drop, you are sent through mind-numbing hill after hill along a 3000-foot track at speeds reaching forty-five miles per hour that leave you wanting more. I noticed that the single lap bar only goes so far down, so no matter who you are, you will feel the intense airtime on this ride. The airtime is phenomenal, and the double up and double down element takes this ride to the next level. This is a coaster experience which true coaster enthusiasts, especially those who love their wood coasters, should not pass up. It is a wild and extremely intense ride. True, there are plenty of bigger, faster coasters around, but this one packs one heck of a punch for its size. The sheer genius of its design makes this coaster consistently appear on many national top ten lists, and so it should.

8 *Shivering Timbers* at Michigan Adventures in Muskegon, Michigan is a wild wooden ride that simply needs to be experienced by everyone. Created at a cost of $4.5 million by Great Coasters International (GCI) in 1998, this coaster is the main reason why you should visit Muskegon. Standing at 125 feet with a 120-foot, fifty-seven-degree drop, this coaster redefines the standard for the out and back concept. At 5384 feet long, this is also one of the longest coasters I have ridden, and at a top speed of fifty-seven miles per hour is surely one of my most memorable. In a word, this coaster is *big* and impressive to look at. The first drop is incredible, and if that weren't enough, it is followed by two more massive hills, each of which provide almost out-of-your-seat standing airtime. There are six hills on the out run and six on the back run, and all twelve produce some of the best airtime and negative-g effects there are. You can also feel the side-slamming intensity of this ride in the final helix. Make sure you ride in both the very front as well as the back of this ride. You will find that each offers a different ride experience to the coaster enthusiast. If you choose the front seat, you will truly experience a whole lot of what I like to call "seat ejection" going over the top of just about every hill, especially on the first three mega-hills. The back seat doesn't have as much airtime over the small hills, but that is more than made up for when you experience those three huge negative-g drops and the whipping action that you will definitely experience from this position. All in all, it's a fabulous coaster and one that you will surely see on everyone's top ten lists for many years to come.

9 *The Beast* at Paramount's Kings Island in Kings Mills, Ohio was the first extraordinary coaster built at the Kings Island complex. Created in 1979 by the Dinn Corporation, the *Beast* stands at 105 feet high but delivers a 135-foot first drop at a forty-five-degree angle, reaching a speed in excess of sixty miles per hour. If the first hill isn't enough for you, it has a second powered hill at 141 feet high that leads to a wicked double helix inside a tunnel which seems to catch everyone's attention. It is here where the ride achieves its rated seventy mph top speed. In my mind this ride is still one of the best traditional wood coasters that you will ever find. You will always find this coaster in the top twenty of just about every national coaster survey taken, and like many, I agree it should be there as well. At 7400-feet long, it's also still the longest and one of the fastest wooden roller coasters in the world. When most rides are ending, this one seems to have just begun. The *Beast* takes advantage of the natural forest terrain as the ride plunges into a tunnel and runs through the woods at consistently high speeds.

I will tell you that this ride at times can be a rough one. I guess age has crept up on this wooden marvel a tad, but rough or not, you will feel your adrenaline increase all through this ride. A must ride for the serious coaster enthusiast, the *Beast* is one you just shouldn't pass up.

10 *The Texas Giant* at Six Flags over Texas is an oversized wooden coaster that really is a joy to experience. At 143-feet high, this woodie was the tallest in the world when it debuted in 1990. The view from the top is exquisite, and the ride itself can be compared to riding a wild bronco, as it streaks down the track at speeds reaching in excess of sixty-five miles per hour. As a twister style coaster, it constantly goes back into its structure, so you are not really able to see the next turn. You will also find that there are many head-chopping effects during its two and a half minute ride cycle. Dinn and Summers really knew what they were doing when they put this ride together. Although several other oversized woodies (like *Hercules* at

The Beast at Paramount's Kings Island in Kings Mills, Ohio

The Texas Giant at Six Flags over Texas

Pete Trabucco

Dorney Park) have been quite disappointing, this *Giant* continues to perform like the champ it really is. As with most wooden coasters, the *Texas Giant* can sometimes be temperamental. Depending on the time of day and weather conditions at the park, this ride varies in its overall intensity, but it is truly an experience for those who love wood coasters. I like riding this monster right at sunset overlooking the big ole Texas horizon. Clearly the *Texas Giant* is why you should come to this park.

11 *Lighting Racer* at Hershey Park in Pennsylvania is a thrill-a-minute wooden coaster, and one that I highly recommend. Hershey Park, known for their outstanding chocolate products, factory tour, and three-dimensional rides, also boasts one heck of an amusement park, if you didn't already know this. Their marquee ride is a wooden coaster created in May of 2000 from the Great Coasters International (GCI) corporation and is a big hit at the park. GCI is known for creating some of the best woodies in the country. Hershey has introduced its brand new type of wood coaster that combines a traditional out and back concept with one of a racing genre. Located at the far end of the Midway America section of the park, *Lightning Racer* stands 90-feet high and has two separate tracks that seem to mirror each other. The two trains race down the first drop together at fifty mph, and at this point the race is won. For the next two and a half minutes, riders will encounter fifteen drops, a few near misses, and an incredible finish that will prompt the rider to cheer for your train over the other. At one point the trains head toward each other at a combined speed of seventy plus mph and almost collide with a waterfall. At the end, computer proximity sensors will declare the winner of the race as you head into the station. It is a great ride, and those who like the feel of a wood coaster will be pretty happy with this one. GCI makes the best woodies around, and in my opinion, this one is the best they have created so far.

12 *The Cyclone* at Astroland Park in Coney Island is still the wooden coaster that has set the standard for all others in the nation. Created in 1927 for a mere $175,000, this coaster still ranks in the top fifteen worldwide, even today, and still packs a wild punch for all those who are lured to it. Located just feet away from the beach, riders get a fantastic view from its eighty-five-foot lift hill before they plunge at sixty miles per hour down one of the steepest first drops, fifty-eight degrees, ever created for a wooden coaster. The *Cyclone* is, in a word, "a classic." From the old style, original bench seats and lap bars to its constant drops, turns and twists, when you ride this coaster, you know you have ridden one of the best in the world! This coaster never seems to slow down through its 3500-foot course, and the ten drops just seem to keep on coming. Since the coaster footprint is small, the g's (both positive and negative) are pretty intense. Famous aviation legend Charles Lindbergh once said that this coaster was "even scarier than flying." If you sit in the very back seat of this contraption, I believe he may have been right. There is also the 1948 story of Emilio Franco, who had an ailment that made it impossible to speak. After a ride on the *Cyclone* he was reported to have spoken his first words, "I feel sick!" The *Cyclone* is one ride that all roller coaster enthusiasts must experience at least once in their lives. It still runs as it did when built and has not been modified to tame it, as many other coasters have. One more thing, after the ride on this Coney Island attraction, you don't even have to leave your seat in order to ride again. Just pay the man as he walks on by and prepare for another sensational ride. Now you just can't beat that!

13 *Rampage* at Visionland in Bessemer, Alabama is without a doubt the highlight of what this park has to offer. At eighty-seven feet high, you do not expect the first drop on this wooden wonder to be a pretty steep 106 feet to the bottom. I am told that this coaster was modeled after *MagaFobia* in Wales, but since I never had the pleasure of riding that coaster, I will

The Cyclone at Astroland Park in Coney Island

America's Top Roller Coasters & Amusement Parks

just have to take their word for it. Built by CCI (who else?) in 1998, *Rampage* is a superb wooden coaster that races around a 3500-foot track at top speeds of fifty-five miles per hour. *Rampage* was also ranked a few years back as a top five wooden coaster in the world, according to a Discovery Channel program on top coasters that year. I think the accolades are definitely well-deserved here! The ride is visually stunning, with a hillside location which can be seen from just about anywhere in the park. One of the best aspects of the ride is that there seems to be no braking other than at the end of this ride, so you get the feeling that you are literally out of control most of the time and accruing mounds and mounds of airtime as you go along. From what I hear, *Rampage* can be very temperamental to some people. I myself loved the ride experience, but if you ask five other people about *Rampage,* at least one person would not share my opinion regarding this woodie. Also, I like visuals when I am riding wooden coasters, but oddly enough, the better ride on *Rampage* seems to be found more in the back section than up front where I

like it. Airtime is good, but it's the lateral movement of this coaster that most people, including myself, seem to remember. A must ride if you ever find yourself in the hills of Alabama.

14 *The Comet* at Six Flags Great Escape Fun Park is, in a word, fantastic. A former nationally top-ranked wooden coaster, *Comet* continues to exhibit the attributes it had in order to receive that highest accolade. The *Comet* was first constructed in 1927 by legendary coaster builder Harry Traver. Back then it was called the *Cyclone,* and it was thought by many to be the most intense coaster ever. It had a laminated wood track with a steel superstructure, but it was considered to be a wooden coaster by definition. At ninety-five feet high with a pretty fair eighty-seven-foot drop, *Comet* seems to get faster and wilder as it rushes down the tracks at over fifty-five miles per hour. A bunny hop heaven with a double out and back setup, the Philadelphia Toboggan Company can be proud of their work here. As you continue through your run, the turns seem to get tighter and there are several unexpected and venomous little side twists en route that will take your breath away. The final turnaround is where this coaster really shines. You seem to be again picking up speed as you enter the final turn-around, and you truly feel like you are about to be ejected out of your seat. This ride packs a punch and if you love negative g's, you will truly love this ride. It has been my experience that the lines are never really too long here, and at this park on most days you will be able to ride again and again to your heart's content. Enjoy!

15 *Twister* at Knobles in Elysburg, Pennsylvania, is another coaster that you should not pass up. Using the drawings of John Allen's and the old *Mr. Twister* from Elitch Gardens, at a cost of $3 million, Knobles has built a fun, exuberating ride that is relentless from start to finish. An instant classic, I guarantee you have not ridden a twister that can compare to this one. With few lateral slams, this one is designed for

fun thrills, not fear. Riders race around the 3900-foot track at over fifty mph, but in this tight space, you get the feeling you are actually moving much faster than that. At 192 feet with a first drop of ninety feet, *Twister* also has an awesome double helix as you go down the second drop. Since the coaster has many of these drops and twists, I believe *Twister* successfully combines two roller coasters into one, and the head-chopper effect on this classic is absolutely magnificent. This one is a good example of a woodie that gets it right with consistent pacing throughout your journey. I also enjoyed the placement of this ride in the park. Nestled in a beautifully wooded area, the coaster looks like it is truly part of the landscape. As with most wood coasters, your experience on this one can vary from day to day, but overall I found it to be an exciting adventure every time I rode it. This is also a classic coaster to ride at night.

16 *Gwazi* at Busch Gardens in Tampa, Florida is the best example of inter-twining two wood coasters together, although from above it is quite difficult to see where one track starts and the other one ends. Adorned by vibrant colors and thematic motifs, both the lion and the tiger coasters set riders hurtling at each other several times during the ride sequence. Great Coasters International put together this dueling coaster in 1999, and since then it has pleased many a finicky coaster fanatic. The secret is in the track itself. You simply have no idea where you are going, or for that matter, where the other track is. Because of this, you constantly look around at track that could be yours or your opponent's. The two coaster tracks are not identical. You get a different ride on the lion than you do on the tiger. The tracks themselves have different personalities as well, depending on when in the day you ride them. I personally like the back row on the tiger but thought the front two seats on the lion were the best. The great thing about roller coasters is that you will always get varying opinions, so to experience firsthand is the only way to go here. At over 3400 feet per track and reaching speeds of fifty miles per hour, you will enjoy the ride.

17 *Great White* at Morey's Pier in Wildwood, New Jersey is a must coaster to ride. One of the two things I most enjoy about *Great White* is that at the top of the 110-foot lift hill, you have an absolutely amazing view of the Atlantic Ocean. The second thing I love about this ride is that after you complete the fifty mile per hour first drop, you will literally feel your body ejecting out of your seat as you enter the turnaround element that directly overlooks the ocean below. All through this ride there are amazing drops and high speed turns and twists, making this 3300-foot marvel very popular among roller coaster enthusiasts. During the ride you will also pass quite close to the nearby sky ride and literally speed down the track while an ocean breeze blasts you in the face. The negative g's experienced on this ride are phenomenal. Another point of interest on *Great White* occurs just after you leave the station, when you will literally go though the floor of the pier itself before you start your climb to the top of the lift hill. This combination twister and double out and back is a destination coaster and is a top attraction at this pay-as-you-go park. It is definitely worth the trip to the Jersey shore.

18 *Giant Dipper* at Belmont Park in San Diego, California is one of those happy testimonials to the preservation of a proven classic ride. Standing but not operating for years (closed in the early '70s, and re-opened in 1990), this marvel was refurbished by the town so that future generations would be able to enjoy this one-of-a-kind ride. This coaster is one of the last remaining Frank Prior & Fred Church coasters ever to be created. Built in 1925, this coaster survived three fires, avoided demolition by the city, and later became a National Historic Landmark. This wooden coaster stands at a mere seventy-three feet high, but don't let the size of this ride fool you. Equipped with flanged wheels, the trains on this wonderful seaside coaster negotiate some remarkable turns and twists over very little straight track all through their 2600-foot run. Reaching speeds as high as fifty-five miles per hour, this coaster is a joy to behold. Like many coasters, the *Giant Dipper* has many different personalities. If it seems a little slow in the morning, go back in the afternoon and you will be positively surprised. Along with the *Giant Dipper* in Santa Cruz and the *Cyclone* in Brooklyn, this coaster is a must-ride for any roller coaster enthusiast looking to experience the classic innovation of these early twister coasters. There is something to be said for wooden coasters built around the ocean that just makes them a cut above the rest. Enjoy and don't forget to check out the open-air market all around this quaint coaster park.

19 *The Wild One* at Six Flags America is a wonderful, classic wooden coaster. This coaster, built by John Miller and the Dinn Corporation stands at ninety-eight feet high and throws its riders off the edge at 53 miles per hour. It is a living testament to the golden era of roller coasters. Six Flags Corporation really did a great thing when they decided to preserve this gem of a woodie. The *Wild One* coaster dates back to 1917. It originally circled along one side of Paragon Park in Hull, Massachusetts, south of Boston, where it was known simply as the *Giant Coaster*. When the seaside park closed (along with so many other vintage amusement parks) in 1985, the Maryland park saved it from the wrecking ball. The *Wild One* stirs the senses with its nostalgic appeal: the look of the rickety, white-painted support beams; the sound of the click-clack-click as the train climbs the lift hill; and the out-of-control feel as riders get tossed from side to side. Even the smell of the grease seems from another era. This traditional ride qualifies as a living piece of history. Airtime abounds throughout the ride, and many times you feel like this ride is going to catapult you out of your seat (but of course you are safely attached to the car's lap bar system, so that won't happen). I defy anyone to emerge from this ride without an ear-to-ear grin. Six Flags America has undergone many changes in recent years, and the *Wild One* has had to conform to those changes. Slightly modified in its ride intensity, this coaster now runs through the skull of the park's water flume and lasts approximately two and a half minutes. There really doesn't seem to be much of a line for this fun coaster. (People are too busy going over the *Superman* or *Batwing*.) So if you want a good quick ride on a classic wood coaster, this is the one for you.

20 *Roar* at Six Flags America was the second wooden coaster created by Great Coasters International. It debuted in May of 1998 and whisks around the twister track at a good fifty miles per hour. What I really like about this coaster is that there are no straight-aways anywhere on this track. The rider is constantly turning, banking, and diving throughout the entire 2300-foot course. Once *Roar's Millennium Flyer* trains are loaded and lap bars secure, the wooden coaster comes to life and three ninety-degree curves lead riders to the lift hill. The chain lift carries the train slowly up to the top of the ninety feet of lift, up and over a twisting, turning layout down below. Once the click-clacking ceases, the train heads straight toward the impossibly tight curvature of a very steep, twisting first drop—and *Roar* wastes no time in navigating the curving drop to the bottom. The track next wraps around the layout's fan curve (a 270-degree inclined spiral), which sends the train into its first camelback hump. After coasting over this element, *Roar* dives back down and takes the passengers up and around another fan curve. Diving down and curving to the left, the coaster speeds over a quick hill and sweeps through a 270-degree banked turn leading into the ride's tunneled section, where the train encounters the layout's steepest banked turn. Exiting the tunnel, there is another curve, and you are now ready for the finale. The trains start their furious run to the brake area with a high-speed curving hop, a complete 180-degree turnaround and one last surprising hop. All told, ten banked curves and twenty-one crisscrosses (under and over) occur on this ride. You can see that after creating the *Wildcat* at Hershey Park, GCI took this concept to the next level. I might add that they succeeded famously here. This is my wife's favorite ride, and I am pretty keen on this one as well. Lines are never that long, so you can ride *Roar* as many times as you like during the day. Try the front row. You will love that first drop!

21 *Puma* at Clementon Park in Clementon, New Jersey is the best kept secret in the roller coaster industry. This monster is a wooden roller coaster designed by S&S Power and built by Philadelphia Toboggan Coasters located at Clementon Amusement Park, and is 2602-feet long. Opened in 2004, its first drop is 105 feet and can take its riders up to fifty-six mph. This $4 million ride is 1 minute 30 seconds from start to finish. Originally named *Tsunami,* in 2005 its name was changed to *J2* to honor the 1919 Jackrabbit (due to protests), which was abandoned in 2002, and because of the 2004 Indian Ocean Tsunami. During parts of the 2005 season and after the season was over, parts of the coasters track was replaced by Great Coasters International to provide a smoother ride. During the 2006 season, the park only operated with one train while the other was worked on by Philadelphia Toboggan Coasters. If you're ever in the Philadelphia area, don't mss this one. It is definitely worth the wait…

22 *The Wildcat* at Hershey Park in Hershey, Pennsylvania, was the first creation for Great Coasters International. It opened in May of 1996 and cost $5 million to complete. Perched at the top of this ninety-foot coaster, you will experience swooping curves and directional changes not experienced on many wood coasters. On *Wildcat* you will also reach top speeds of 50 miles per hour and will wonder where the next turn is. The ride is situated on two acres of land and is 3,183 feet of pure adrenaline. *Wildcat* reaches a top speed of 50 miles per hour while it crosses its path twenty times. During this ride you get the feeling of constant acceleration and relentless curves throughout the course. On *Wildcat* you enter the course at pretty much the same speed as when you started. You come into the last turn at a startling 40 miles per hour. The ride provides great airtime, but the unusual layout is what makes this a great coaster. There are literally no straight portions on this track. Its layout is a throwback to earlier times and like its successor, *Roar* at Six Flags America, it gives a stunning nostalgic experience. Riding *Wildcat* is about as close as you can come to experiencing what it was like to ride the old classics from another age. Ride cars built by the Philadelphia Toboggan Company are comfortable and feature individual ratcheting, lap bars, and a headrest. As on most twisters, ride the front and after the first hill, watch the actual frame of this ride sway as you enter the next element. You will truly believe this *CAT* is alive. Since day one this has been a popular ride with many roller coaster enthusiasts.

23 *The Riverside Cyclone* at Six Flags New England is simply one great ride. Standing at over one hundred feet tall, this coaster might have debuted in 1983, but just one look at its beauty, and you would swear it was a product of the 1920's and 30's. Created by Bill Cobb, this coaster is known for its amazing drops

Pete Trabucco

Puma at Clementon Park in Clementon, New Jersey

and tight turns. In 2001 the first drop was modified and shortened by fifteen to twenty feet. In my mind, this in no way changes the ride in the least. What I like about this, *Cyclone* is its amazing second drop and tight turning action. It's a newer coaster with the classic coaster feel. It also is a coaster that can be finicky with its riders. Sometimes you just get a good ride, but at other times, sometimes on the same day, you will get the ride of your life as you streak along the 3400-foot long course. Depending on the time of day and atmospheric conditions, as well as what train you get, this coaster can be potentially one of the fiercest coasters you will ever ride, especially if you sit in the back seat. This might be a new-generation wood coaster, but it has the unmistakable feel of an older coaster, and one that I would label "classic." It always ranks among enthusiasts' favorites due to its tight turns, sudden drops and disorienting nature. In 2000, brand new Philadelphia Toboggan Company retired the aging Morgan trains, which had replaced the original PTC's in the 1980s. This ride is truly a masterpiece and one that you will enjoy with most of your family. Seating is first come first serve. Very rarely are there long lines waiting for this ride, perhaps because the entrance is off the beaten trail, so unless you really are looking for it, you might just miss it.

24 *Rebel Yell* at Paramount's Kings Dominion has been featured in many movies in the late '70s and '80s. It also is the site where American Coaster Enthusiasts (ACE) was originally formed. *Rebel Yell* might be a standard out and back racing coaster, but it does have a twist. Its claim to fame in the coaster world is that one of the racing trains runs backward. This was a great change, adding some excitement to an old coaster that might otherwise be overlooked today. What an odd feeling to go up a hill and have no idea when you were going to stop! Both trains seem to rush headlong to the finish, and you never do know until the end which car is going to win. Built in 1975 by the Philadelphia Toboggan Company, the train speeds around the dual course at fifty-five miles per

Pete Trabucco

hour along a 3368-foot track. The view at the top of the eighty-five-foot lift hill is splendid, and the coaster still performs like a trooper. Lines are never really long, and I recommend that you ride the cars forward and backward for your own comparison. If you like a consistent, old-style wooden race coaster, this ride is for you.

25 *Thunderhawk* at Dorney Park in Allentown, Pennsylvania is one ride you will not soon forget. Built in 1923, this wooden coaster is one of the oldest in the country and races down the track at speeds reaching forty-five miles per hour. *Thunderhawk* is a classic crowd-pleaser, once known simply as *The Coaster*. An initial sixty-five-foot plunge launches riders on a high-speed journey complemented by unpredictable twists and incredible airtime all through its 2700-foot run. It provides tons of lateral g's, great head-chopper effects and some very nice airtime. One thing I did notice was the trim on the second to last bunny hill coming in to the station. It slows the ride

down way too quickly and spoils what could be a great ending. The *Thunderhawk* was designed and built with pressure-treated Southern Pine by the Philadelphia Toboggan Company. The design of the coaster today is a bit different from when the out and back coaster was first created. It was designed by the legendary Herb Schmeck (who worked for none other than John Miller) and was converted to a figure eight design in 1930. On some days this ride can wreak havoc on your body and yet on other days, you will truly get the ride of your life. This is one coaster where sitting in the back seat is equivalent to going fifteen rounds with a heavyweight boxer. I loved it anyway.

26 *Thunderbolt* at Six Flags New England was built in 1941, just one year after the flyer *Comet* at Whalon Park. The *Thunderbolt* has a surprising element that very few coasters have a double-dip drop series. This means that as you drop, you stop, level off, and then drop again. It is a great experience for those who have never tried this type of element before. The coaster is a classic and one that delivers a consistent ride every time. For new coaster fanatics and families alike, this is the one you should ride. Take advantage of *Thunderbolt* and ride this vintage family woodie at night. You will be happy you did, so will your son or daughter.

27 *The Comet* at Hershey Park, Hershey, Pennsylvania, is a great classic wooden coaster. This ride has a seventy-eight-foot drop and reaches a top speed of fifty mph. The coaster dates back to 1946 and at the time was one of the biggest coasters ever created. Designed by Herbert Schmeck and built by the Philadelphia Toboggan Company, this coaster is a modified double out and back design. I especially like the first drop suspended over water. This drop sends riders into a hairpin turn before it drops you again on your way to very nice ride experience. It creaks, cracks and looks rickety, but in my opinion is a gem of a coaster and one that all coaster aficionados should try.

28 *Rolling Thunder* at Six Flags Great Adventure, Jackson, New Jersey, still holds a place in my heart. You never forget the first real roller coaster you ride, and this one was mine. By today's standards, *Rolling Thunder* is not much to speak of, but even though it was created over twenty-five years ago, it still thrills and delights all those who ride the *Thunder*. This ninety-six-foot out and back wooden coaster races over hills and has dual tracks. Unlike other racers, the courses are different so you actually get two rides in one. Each track was created differently and offers a distinctive and uniquely different ride experience. The right side is tamer and allows the riders to enjoy the view a bit more. However, the left side has clearly the best drops and offers much more airtime to its passengers. One observation I have made about *Rolling Thunder* is that it is one of the loudest screeching coasters ever created. The lack of oil on the rails has given *RT* the nickname "Screeching Thunder," and after riding it, you will see why. On busy days, both trains will run simultaneously, and although not as intense as

Pete Trabucco

the generation racers running today, it is still a good family coaster to ride. The sensation of being lifted out of your seat during the 3200-foot course, while reaching speeds of fifty-five miles per hour, is quite common on *Rolling Thunder's* left side, so if this does not appeal to you, go to the right and directly up the stairs as soon as you enter the queue. The lap bars are old and the paint is peeling everywhere (in 2003 they finally painted the whole ride), but in my mind, this only makes *Rolling Thunder* more of a classic old-style racer and adds to its overall appeal.

29 *The Dragon Coaster* at Playland Park, Rye, New York was built in 1929, just after the park debut. It was built by Fred Church and is one of the last remaining examples of his work. This is a very interesting ride with a unique V-shaped layout. Standing at seventy-five feet tall with a sixty-foot drop, riders fly down the 3400-foot track at speeds reaching forty-five miles per hour. You might notice that the ride seems a little longer than it actually is. This is achieved by *Dragon* being a multilayered coaster, so just when you expect the ride to end, you have another section of track to cover. This coaster has been featured in many movies, and one of its more memorable moments occurs when you get to go through the dragon's mouth and out its tail. A classic coaster and one you should experience. Note: Playland Park is a pay-as-you-go park, so you can ride this one many times without notice of any long lines.

30 *The Jack Rabbit Coaster* at Clementon Park, New Jersey, was built in 1917 and is the second-oldest operational coaster in the country. In fact, there is only one coaster in America that can boast to being older (*Leap for Dips* which was created in 1902). Standing at fifty feet high and overlooking most of the park, this ride shoots you down several hills at speeds that reach thirty-eight miles per hour. Created by the legend himself, John Miller, this 1700-foot figure eight design operated with trains with no up-stops, which unfortunately limited the experience quite a bit. However, new trains were added in 1999, and the ride is much better and wilder than it was. It is truly a family coaster and one that the whole family will enjoy. Since trees, foliage, and other rides hide most of the coaster, those who want a preview before they ride it should go on the little park train first to give you a better perspective of the ride itself. But beware! There are elephants, bears and other wild animals roaming around this area. You will know that they are not real as you ride by them, by the paint that seems to be peeling off most of them. Still, the kids will enjoy this ride. *The Jack Rabbit* is a fast and enjoyable little woodie, and one that I highly recommend. You kind of get the feeling that, if this ride could talk, oh, the stories it might be able to tell you…

Even though this ride is no longer operating, I have to mention that it was a great ride and I hope that one day, the new owners of Clementon Park put this coaster back into full operation.

Pete Trabucco

Top Amusement Parks (in America)

Like the roller coasters they house, there are literally hundreds of amusement parks around the country. They all provide a service in family entertainment that is extremely important to all who enter their gates. There are, however, some amusement parks that are simply better than the rest. At these parks, you are not only entering a place of escape but are preparing for an experience that you will not soon forget. When I chose the following locations, I took into account many different aspects. Thrills and top water rides are important but not the entire picture. Food, overall price, the park's accessibility, shows, and many other aspects go into making a great park. I also tried to make sure that for those who want to experience the best amusement parks the nation has to offer, you could find one that was local to your area. Please remember, these are *my* picks for the top amusement parks. In the end, your opinion is the sole reason why you visit a park in the first place. Enjoy my list (listed alphabetically) and compare it to yours!

1. Astroland and Deno's Wonderwheel Park
2. Busch Gardens (Europe) Williamsburg
3. Busch Gardens (Africa) Tampa
4. Cedar Point
5. Disneyland/California Adventure
6. Dorney Park and Wildwater Kingdom
7. Hershey Park, Pennsylvania
8. Knott's Berry Farm

9. Knoebels Amusement Park

10. Lake Compounce

11. Michigan Adventure

12. Morey's Piers

13. Paramount's Kings Dominion

14. Paramount's Kings Island

15. SeaWorld Florida

16. Six Flags America

17. Six Flags Great Adventure

18. Six Flags—Great Escape

19. Six Flags Magic Mountain

20. Six Flags New England

21. Six Flags over Texas

22. Universal Studios Florida

23. Universal Studio's Islands of Adventure

24. Walt Disney World

25. Wonderland Park-Canada

1 *Astroland and Deno's Wonderwheel Park.* There's no shortage of excitement at Coney Island in the summertime. All of the rides and games at Astroland and Deno's Wonderwheel Park (as well as some of the smaller parks here at Coney Island) will have you rushing this way and that way all day. It is truly a New York experience, and as a native New Yorker, it is one that I certainly can relate to. But you don't have to be a native New Yorker to enjoy. Are these big parks? Will you find the most thrilling rides here? The answer to both questions is no, but what you will find is the atmosphere and old world charm of the place where the concept of modern-day amusement parks was created. This is the place where the very first modern-day coasters came into existence, the *Switchback Railway* being the nation's first modern-day coaster. Also the infamous *Tornado* once stood here, and of course this is still where the mother of all wooden coasters still resides.

Sure, there are many new wooden coasters that can claim to be taller, faster, and longer, but nothing

Pete Trabucco

can take away the title of "most infamous coaster on the planet" held by the Coney Island *Cyclone.* Here you will still find the world-renowned and still operational coaster at Coney Island since its birth in 1927, and still packing a mighty punch for its size. After all, this is the coaster that noted aviator Charles Lindbergh once said was "scarier than flying."

At Coney Island you can also visit the place where you get the *original* Nathan's hot dogs, the best hot dogs that you will ever taste. The building has been around longer than the *Cyclone* and still draws bigger lines than any other attraction in the area. Get a side of fries with the hot dog, and you will be in junk food heaven!

Also, Deno's *The Wonderwheel* is one of only two Ferris wheels in the world whose chairs slide back and forth. When you get to the top, the gondolas inch forward and slide across a path that will make you think you're going right off the edge! My pick for the best and scariest Ferris wheel in the world is this one. It also provides a great view of the beach,

although the best view can be obtained on the 300-foot *Astrotower* right next to the *Cyclone* coaster.

At both parks, you pay as you go, and the price for the top rides is very affordable. There used to be a real problem with gangs and crime in the area. But since the new urban renewal program and the creation of a new minor league baseball team, it is a place I feel comfortable taking my family to. That's right, between your park hopping, you will be able to watch a free ballgame from a minor league baseball team aptly named the "Brooklyn Cyclones."

Finally, if you are a beach lover, this is a place to go in the city where you can fly kites and run through the sand. You can find "polar bears" (the human kind), fishermen, sand sculptors, ice skaters, muscle men, sword swallowers, strollers, thrill seekers, old-timers, and sightseers of all sorts at the Brooklyn shore as well. You will even find the New York Aquarium not too far away. It is worth the day to visit the island—Coney Island that is! Rumor has it that this classic park might be on the chopping block. I sincerely hope this doesn't happen for if it does, a big piece of coaster history will surely be lost forever.

2 *Busch Gardens Tampa* Busch Gardens Tampa, Florida, is an African theme park offering a small, but pretty thrilling selection of coasters with a large selection of animals that you and your kids will love. In fact, it features one of the country's premier zoos (the sixth largest in the world) with more than 2700 animals, as well as a good variety of live shows, exhibits, restaurants, and shops. The park is divided into several themed areas based on countries from the African continent. The themes are very convincing and interesting. Among the park's non-coaster attractions is The Serengeti Plain, a twenty nine-acre nature reserve that everyone in your family will really enjoy. Also, taking a trip on to Busch Garden's latest attraction, *Rhino Rally* lets you get real close to the numerous elephants, rhinos zebras, antelope and hundreds of other species in the park. Here, man is the visitor and the animals roam free. The reserve can also be experienced free via the train or skyride, or by a guided truck tour for an additional cost. This is a park with plenty to do for everyone, including a very limited selection of nicely themed flat rides which include three water rides, a very short log flume, and a fairly tame river rapid. Plus you get five world-class coasters (six if you count *Gwazi's* two tracks). All this and a great educational experience for those who love animals, (and let's not forget the great shops). Overall, the park is very clean, like its sister park in Virginia, and is well-maintained. The staff is friendly, and for the most part, knowledgeable. Prices are competitive with the nearby parks, but the crowds are usually lighter than the ones you will find an hour to the east in Florida's Orlando parks.

Along with the newer *Islands of Adventure,* Busch Gardens Tampa has some great coasters. Both *Kumba* and *Montu* have been rated as two of the best steel coasters in the world, and I can tell you they truly are. These coasters are the main reason why coaster aficionados come to this park. But let's not forget that most patrons also visit this park to see the animals, birds, reptiles and mammals that are a showcase you can't find at many other parks. I really like this park! So will you!

3 *Busch Gardens Williamsburg* in Virginia is not only a theme park but a unique experience for the whole family. It is an action-packed, European-themed park combining seventeenth century charm and twenty-first century technology. It boasts of more than one hundred acres of unparalleled fun and adventure for the entire family. This is one of the most aesthetic parks in the country. With more than forty thrilling rides and attractions, eight main stage shows, a wide variety of authentic foods and shops, plus an enchanting children's area. Busch Gardens Williamsburg is the ticket to a world-class adventure. Busch Gardens has been voted the world's "Most Beautiful Theme Park" for the tenth consecutive year by the National Amusement Park Historical Association (NAPHA), and that in itself is a feat. NAPHA has named Busch Gardens Williamsburg the world's most "Favorite Theme Park" as well. If that isn't enough, Busch Gardens has also received many *Amusement Today* accolades in the categories of "Best Landscape," "Best Food," and "Cleanest" in the nation. Also, the park recently received the prestigious Applause Award from the International Association of Amusement Parks & Attractions (IAAPA) and *Amusement Business Magazine*. If you're a coaster enthusiast, you'll love this park because it also holds five great roller coasters, two of which are the best of their type around the country. They are *Alpengeist*, the tallest suspended coaster in the world, and of course the world-famous *Apollo's Chariot*, a thrill a minute, two hundred-foot hypercoaster. New this year at the Williamsburg adventure park is R.L. Stine's attraction, *Haunted Lighthouse 4-D*, which combines state-of-the-art visual effects with multisensory surprises. Special effects such as interactive seats engage the audience in an extraordinary experience. Guests can also enjoy a variety of options with two, three, and four day bounce tickets. This means that visitors can enjoy Busch Gardens, bounce over to Water Country USA, and then bounce back to the park. And you can do this all day long, a great feature if you have really small kids. The great thing about Busch Gardens is that you don't need to be a coaster lover to really enjoy this park. True, the rides are first-class, but with your one-price ticket, you get shows that are spectacular. The staff is always friendly and the food is also pretty good. My top pick for everyone in the family.

4 *Cedar Point* in Sandusky, Ohio is America's second-oldest remaining amusement park and is without a doubt the largest single standing park in America. Having opened to the public back in 1870, it is located on a picturesque peninsula jutting out onto Lake Erie and is approximately halfway between Toledo and Cleveland, Ohio. Millions of people flock religiously to this park every year. Cedar Point is a park that has been literally handmade for the coaster enthusiast. With sixteen world-class roller coasters (most of them the best in their particular categories), Cedar Point can take the average coaster fanatic days to experience every ride that this park has to offer. My advice is to take your time and enjoy the sixty plus rides in the park.

In addition to the award-winning rides, you will find some of the best shows and food that you can find at an amusement park. With all this going on, make it a point not to rush. Besides, the *Point* now has a ride reservation system, utilizing hand stamps, called the "freeway," where you can ride the hot attractions without paying an extra fee. It is available on *Millennium Force, Magnum, Mantis, Raptor* and *Wicked Twister*. All you have to do is go to the Freeway hand stamp booth located near the ride entrance and get your hand stamped with a boarding time. Your boarding time is good for one ride anytime within the one hour stamped on your hand. When you're ready to ride, just show your hand stamp to the ride host at the entrance to the ride, and you will enter the freeway queue, which merges with the regular ride queue just minutes before entering any station. At this point a ride host will stamp "ride" on your hand to indicate that you have used your boarding time. It's that easy!

Cedar Point, known for its world-record-breaking roller coasters, did it again in 2003. *Top Thrill Dragster* is now the tallest, fastest roller coaster on the planet and well worth the wait (which at times can be very long)! On this ride, you literally get shot out of the station, climb 420 feet, and ascend at speeds of over 120 mph. The pucker factor, ladies and gentlemen, on this ride has now made it the one that all other rides must match, and I tell you, folks, that ain't easy. It has literally taken the thrill experience up to a new level. *Top Thrill Dragster* is not for the faint of heart, nor is it for the average coaster enthusiast, so beware.

Adjacent to Cedar Point is Soak City, a gigantic eighteen-acre water park featuring action-packed body and inner tube slides, including the mammoth *Zoom Flume,* two meandering inner tube rivers, and a fun-filled play area for kids. It also has an enormous 500,000-gallon wave pool. So all in all, you get top coasters, fantastic views of Lake Erie, great shows, and so much more at the #1 park in the country. It is without a doubt the Mecca of all coaster parks and one not to be missed.

5 *Disneyland* in Anaheim, California really needs no introduction. Walt Disney really revolutionized the amusement park industry when he opened Disneyland in 1955. He wanted to create a themed place "where parents and children could have fun together," and he certainly achieved that goal. Disneyland and Walt Disney World in Florida simply obliterate the nearest competition in terms of popularity and overall attendance. Not only that, these Disney parks have set many standards which all other parks shoot for and very few ever achieve.

The park might be small compared to its counterpart in Florida, but don't let that fool you. It still manages to captivate people and draw over twelve million park visitors a year. The key to Disneyland's success is its staff, customer service program, and total quality management strategy. The rides and shows for the kids are in a league of their own, using the latest technology and animatronics that even today look realistic. There is so much to do and see here. If you are a coaster fanatic, you might not find the most thrilling rides here, but you will be very impressed by the extraordinary themes and outstanding illusion. *Space Mountain* is still one of the best enclosed coasters to date, not for its intensity but as an end result of the overall package, and I have never met a person who didn't enjoy this ride. Another attraction worth riding is the *Runaway Mine Train.* Family coaster enthusiasts will like this one.

Also because of its size, *Disneyland* makes you really feel like you're a part of the action. It is much smaller than the *World* in Florida, and quaint. The original *Matterhorn Bobsleds,* the first steel track coaster, created in 1959, can be found here and is a scaled-down version of the of the actual Matterhorn mountain located in Switzerland. Kids as well as adults love this ride, and over the years a new generation (including my daughter) feels the same way. And let's not forget *Splash Mountain,* maybe not quite as intense as *Splash Mountain* in Florida, but still an e-ticket ride in my book.

Until recently Disneyland stood alone on a seventy-five-acre lot, but now it has a new neighbor, California Adventures, and this park has certainly brought the *Land* into the new millennium. As in Florida, you now have another park, along with a slew of new rides to choose from. These include the top coaster, *California Screaming,* a ride that will take your breath away as well as a drop tower that will scare the daylights out of you. If you haven't visited Disneyland or California Adventures in California, now would definitely be the time to do it.

6 *Dorney Park* in Allentown, Pennsylvania (Cedar Point's sister park) has some of the best rides and attractions that you will find on the east coast. Dorney Park & Wildwater Kingdom's two-hundred acres are home to more than one hundred rides and attractions, including eight roller coasters and dozens of state-of-the-art thrill machines, as well as a water park that is second to none. You will find one of the tallest and fastest coasters in the world right here at Dorney. The two

Pete Trabucco

Talon at Dorney Park in Allentown, Pennsylvania

hundred-foot plus mega coaster *Steel Force* glistens in the sky, and if you like loops and spins, then why not take a ride on the tallest inverted coaster on the east coast, *Talon?* You also can ride the small but feisty *Lazer* coaster, a Schwarzkopf classic, and for wooden coaster enthusiasts, there is the 1923 classic, *Thunderhawk.* For the kids, there are wild mouse rides, *Little Lazer* and *Dragon Coaster.* Finally, look for another stunning 13 million dollar coaster, that has replaced Hercules, called *Hydra The Revenge.*

All Dorney coasters are built to thrill you, whether you are seven or seventy. Also at Dorney Park you will find an authentic 1921 carousel ride and an old-fashioned steam engine that takes you around the park. If you like heights, why not ride the *Dominator,* a tall monstrosity combining a 170-foot drop and ejection tower? And let's not forget Camp Snoopy—the only place on the east coast where families can visit Snoopy, Charlie Brown, and the *Peanuts* gang.

What I really like about this park is that there is action happening everywhere, and the hilly terrain gives the visitor some really nice views of the park. At *Whitewater Rapids,* you will find a state-of-the-art wave pool, and some steep, fast water tube rides, some that start your descent from as high as 70 feet above the tarmac. When you get hungry (and you will), you can choose from more than forty food locations throughout the park. The park also has live shows for everyone. Their staff are not the friendliest people you will find, but overall the rides, shows and water attractions are well worth the price of your admission.

7 *Hershey Park* in Hershey, Pennsylvania is an amusement park that combines wild roller coasters, exciting shows, and the best candy your taste buds can experience. Chocolate magnate Milton Hershey in 1903 founded the town which today has not only a world-class chocolate factory and amusement park, but several professional sports teams as well (soccer and hockey). Also, just outside the park, Hershey has added a new sensational chocolate factory ride, a Muppet-style 3D show for

Pete Trabucco

the kids. In Hershey, Pennsylvania, you will find street lamps shaped like Hershey kisses, a fine 5-star hotel, a golf course or two, and of course, the award-winning park itself.

When you enter the gates of this nicely laid out (but a little hilly) park, you surely know that you have come to one of the sweetest places on earth. There is candy everywhere! Also, you will find several of the nation's top roller coasters in the country. You should start your trip by visiting Chocolate World, the gift shop, and while there checking out the 3D movie. After your chocolate tour, burn off those candy bars with a trip to the park itself. At Hershey Park, you will find twenty kiddy rides and eight stellar roller coasters to choose from. A ninth coaster is scheduled to be added to their collection in the near future, an exciting LIM coaster.

For wooden coaster lovers there are three winners to choose from. If you like to race, then your best choice is *Lightning Racer,* a coaster that really brings out the competitiveness in everyone. The *Wildcat* will also amaze you with countless twists and turns through the course. And if you're looking for a wooden classic, then the *Comet* is your choice.

If steel is your deal, they don't come any better or more intense than *Great Bear* and *Sidewinder.* And if you want to get drenched, then Hershey's newest addition, the *Super Soaker* ("all wet") coaster is for you. You will also find the classic *Superdooperlooper* still in action here, and if you want to ride a real *Wild Mouse,* you can do so here. Also, there is an eleven-acre walk through the zoo that was once Milton Hershey's personal animal collection. The park is clean and well maintained. It is logically laid out with just about the right mixture of attractions, food courts, shops, and displays throughout the park. If you have the time, then Hershey is truly one great vacation hot spot for the entire family.

8 *Knott's Berry Farm,* Buena Park, California is a booming, 160-acre California theme park that started out as a small twenty-acre family berry farm, but this is exactly what happened. Walter and Cornelia Knott bought Knott's Berry Farm during the Depression and began their business way back then. They sold berries, jams, and chicken dinners in order to make ends meet, and just eight decades later, Knott's Berry Farm is undisputed as one of the premiere amusement parks in the nation. With more than 150 attractions (including seven top coasters), restaurants and shops scattered through six themed areas, Knott's Berry Farm is a destination park for just about everyone. Toddlers and elementary schoolers love the shows and rides in Camp Snoopy, while older children and adults get a kick out of the thrill rides in *Wild Water Wilderness* and on the *Boardwalk*. Don't miss *Old West Ghost Town*, historically, the epicenter of the park itself. One of the best wooden coasters ever built, and one of the park's most popular attractions, resides at this location. Its name? *Ghostrider*. *Ghostrider* is an award-winning wooden roller coaster that opened in 1998 and truly needs to be ridden to be believed. Other great coasters include *Xcelerator* and the family coaster *Jaguar*. When the temperature climbs, cool off at the one of the world's most high riding and

steep rides in the world, *Perilous Plunge*. Now that is a serious water ride for the serious thrill-seeker. It is the steepest flume ride every created.

One of the best times to visit this park is in October, when Knott's Berry Farm transforms itself into *Knott's Scary Farm,* a fright fest that almost every other park has tried to copy. Get there and see the park. You will be glad you did! And if you tire of Knott's, just minutes away is another classic park. Most everyone knows it as Disneyland!

9 *Knoebels* in Elysburg, Pennsylvania, made my top park list simply because it is an old-style park with many great rides and unique attractions that you just don't see any more. Comfortably nestled in the picturesque mountains of north central Pennsylvania, Knoebels Amusement Park has been a popular family destination for more than three-quarters of a century. Officially, Knoebels opened in 1926 as Knoebels Amusement Resort.

Today, Knoebels has over fifty rides and attractions, including two of the best wooden coasters you will

Pete Trabucco

find anywhere. First, there is the *Phoenix*, built in 1940 by PTC/Herb Schmeck and named *Rocket* when it resided at Playland Park in San Antonio, Texas. It became a classic in the park when it was relocated to its present site in 1985. All true roller coaster enthusiasts flock to this park in order to ride this wooden wonder.

You will find another woodie by the name of *Twister* here as well. The *Twister* is sure to give you an extreme ride with all the excitement you would expect from a world-class coaster. From over one hundred feet you can experience some pretty good vertical drops, multiple twists and hairpin turns throughout the ride. Both coasters are constantly on the top twenty-five lists around the country.

Then there is *Whirlwind*, a classic Arrow cork-screw coaster just right for those budding coaster aficionados, and finally, *The High Speed Thrill Coaster* built by the Overland Amusement Company of Saugus, Massachusetts. It first opened in 1955 and is believed to be the only operating "Overland coaster" left in the world.

If coasters aren't your thing, why not catch the brass ring on one of the largest and oldest carousels in the world? The *Grand Carousel* was built in 1912. Its sixty-three horses were hand-carved by Master Carver George Carmel and used a Looff machine to spin the ride. Knoebels bought the carousel in the first week of December 1941, and it is one of the few parks left that still offer the brass ring for a free ride! In truth the charm of this park really resides in the many old and classic rides that you just won't find elsewhere.

And you can't come to Knoebels without discovering one of the best dark rides in the nation. Their *Haunted Mansion*, which in many ways rivals Disney's *Haunted Mansion*, is a must see in this park. The Knoebel family marked the park's seventy-seventh anniversary season with the introduction of several new rides, but one really stands out: the new *Scenic Skyway*, a triple-chair ski lift that takes guests on a fourteen minute round trip 364 feet to the top of a mountain near the park's main entrance. It gives you truly one of the best views of the park you can get, and at times it can get pretty steep. It is in fact one of the steepest (49.7 degrees) ski lift rides in the country. For those who don't like heights, this can be the scariest ride at the park.

Finally, if getting wet is what you like to do, there is always Knoebels' *Crystal Pool* with four water slides (not the most modern waterslides around, but still refreshing) that will be sure to please you. Pay-one-price plans are available Monday-Friday during the in-season. Weekends are pay-as-you-go!

10 *Lake Compounce* in beautiful Bristol, Connecticut can boast being the oldest operating amusement park in the United States. The park opened in October of 1846 and still offers the public a place to unwind and escape the realities of everyday life. Its picturesque lake still is home to many wild animals and birds of all kinds. And the sky ride, which takes you 750 feet up to the top of a nearby mountain range, offers an absolutely breathtaking view. In April, 1996, the Kennywood Entertainment Company became the managing partner of Lake Compounce. Since then, this park has seen nearly $50 million in new rides, attractions, and physical improvements added to the park. The park's transformation tastefully integrates its natural beauty and rich heritage with a blend of classic and contemporary rides, live shows, and unique attractions. As Lake Compounce, the nation's first amusement park still in operation continues into the new millennium, a balance between change and tradition continues to be important. From its vintage 1911 carousel, to one of the best wooden coasters ever created in *Boulder Dash,* you must make time for this park. The other coasters, *Wildcat, Zoomerang,* and the kiddy coaster, are also well worth riding. The park's modern shows and attractions, plus a pleasure walk around the lake (that records life on the earth and how short a time period man has reigned supreme on this planet), are real eye-openers and very educational.

Also, on those really hot days, you can cool off on the *Thunder Rapids* raft ride.

Or check out Splash Harbor, Connecticut's only

water park! There, you will find plenty of fun-filled water slides to get the whole family wet! The latest addition to the park is *Mammoth Falls,* a family raft ride that is sure to be wet and wild, with a total drop of over fifty feet through a five hundred-foot course.

11 *Michigan Adventure* may not be the biggest park around, but in my opinion, it has plenty to offer the entire family. Part of the Cedar Fair group (Cedar Point, Knott's Berry Farm, Worlds of Fun, Valleyfair and Dorney Park), Michigan Adventure boasts over fifty rides and attractions and is a great place to have fun and get really wet. At the top of the ride list is *Shivering Timbers,* a world-class coaster with drops of 125, 105, and ninety-five feet in its repertoire of thrill elements, truly one of the best wooden coasters ever put on this planet. If you are a wooden coaster fanatic, you have not ridden the best until you ride this one. Year after year, this coaster manages to be on everyone's top ten list.

Other good coasters to check out are *Wolverine Wildcat,* a Curtis and Summers design, and of course the ACE family classic, *Zach's Zoomer* from Great Coasters International. Also at *Michigan Adventure* you will find the colorful *Mad Mouse* coaster; perfect for the whole family, and the Arrow *Corkscrew* classic. For the kids, Michigan Adventure recently added the *Big Dipper,* a family coaster from Chance rides that is a real hit with the little ones! And let's not forget *Ripcord!* For a few extra bucks you can take a flight from the top of a 173-foot tower at speeds that can reach up to sixty-five mph.

For water lovers, you have a choice of not one but three wave pools and a total of twenty-one water slides. If thrills and attractions aren't your thing, you will find a miniature golf course, lots of food stands, and many different gift shops all over the park to keep you busy. Okay, this one may not be the biggest or most exciting park around, but what puts this one on my list are the people and the overall atmosphere you get from visiting this park. The pace is a little slower here than in most places, but after a busy day in conferences, I surely enjoyed my visit. I am sure you will too.

12 *Morey's Piers* in Wildwood, New Jersey. Now here on the southern shores of New Jersey you will find the largest and most exciting set of amusement piers in the world! The beautiful beaches and Wildwood's famous boardwalk are the backdrop for three incredible fun-filled piers offering seven decent coasters, including wooden marvel *Great White,* the *Great Nor'Easter,* and the *Sea Serpent.* You will also find family-style coasters, such as the *Rollies, Doo Wopper* and *Flitzer.* When you add this to the beautiful beachfront water parks and family rides, plus over two miles of boardwalk, you are truly in for an experience.

Morey's Piers have been bringing thrills and laughter to families for over thirty years, and they seem to be expanding every year. In 1985, *Raging Waters* water park made its debut at the oceanfront end of Mariner's Landing, and following in the footsteps of its success, a second *Raging Waters* opened at Morey's Piers back in 1988. This coincided with the purchase of a third pier, Fun Pier, which was renamed Wildwheels, home to one of the largest Ferris wheels in the country.

Morey's Piers currently feature over 150 pay-as-you-go rides and attractions, hosting over three and a half million visitors per year. The staff, for the most part, are also very interesting characters. Most are college students who come from around the world and work in the states during their summer breaks. The Piers do have a very odd rule of no hats or glasses on the majority of top thrill rides for safety purposes and even have horse-collar restraints on some of the small coasters, but overall, it is a pleasant park. For an added experience and nominal fee you can also ride the *tramcar* up and down the two-mile boardwalk, enjoying one of the most long and pristine beaches on the east coast. All in all, you will have a great time at Morey's Piers, but be warned that during the height of summer, this place gets really crowded!

13 *Paramount's Kings Dominion* is one of the best theme parks on the east coast! You will find some of the most hair-raising rides, including twelve decent roller coasters, the wettest water park, and stunning, innovative stage shows around. There are seven sections to this park, and it is safe to say that there is literally something here for just about everyone. If you are a roller coaster fanatic like I am, you can visit the land of the Congo for *Anaconda, Flight of Fear, Avalanche,* and one of my favorites, *Volcano.* In the Grove section get set for other top coasters such as *Hypersonic XLC,* the *Rebel Yell, Hurler,* and *Shockwave.* In the Old Virginia area of the park, you will find the wooden marvel *Grizzly,* and for kids, Nickelodeon Central, and Kidsville, site of the infamous *Scooby Doo* roller coaster. On International Street you will be able to look over the park on a one-third scale, three hundred-foot model of the Eiffel Tower. And then there is the Water Works section of the park, nineteen acres of cool fun for the whole family, for those who just want cool off and get away from it all.

New is *Kings Dominion's* drop zone stunt tower. At 305-feet tall, it is the tallest drop ride in North America, promising daring riders a 272-foot descent at seventy-two miles per hour! This adrenaline-pumping adventure simulates the sensation of skydiving, offering to the public something new at this four hundred-acre one-of-a-kind theme park. You will enjoy this park, but take your time. You will need a few days to complete your task. It is a pretty big one!

14 *Paramount's Kings Island* near Cincinnati, Ohio has a lot to offer just about everyone. There are great daily shows, Paramount characters, and even an amazing miniature Eiffel tower, which at three hundred feet, is a third the size of the original. You can take a scenic elevator ride to the top of this tower for some awesome open views of the countryside. Overall, you will find more than eighty rides and attractions at Kings Island, with something for every member of the family! You will also find a great whitewater ride in *Whitewater Canyon,* perfect for cooling off on those long hot days.

I think by far, however, Kings Island excels in their roller coaster category. For the kids, there's a small roller coaster called the *Beastie* and a new coaster called *Rugrats, Runaway Reptar.* This ride is an incredible, one-of-a kind suspended kids' coaster that your children will just love. Here you and your little ones get to hang on with Tommy Pickles, Chuckie, and the rest of the *Rugrats* gang as they swoop, twist and turn with the king (Nick) dinosaurs.

Moving up the scale, you have the *Red and Blue Racers,* which run on side-by-side tracks. One of them goes *backward* pretty darn fast. You might remember this ride from an episode of the *Brady Bunch* where this coaster was headlined.

The *Vortex* is an intense metal coaster which features six inversions, one of which is a corkscrew. There is also a stand-up coaster called the *King Cobra,* which was the first stand-up coaster to feature a loop de loop. One of the newer coasters at the park is a suspended coaster called *Top Gun,* a *very* smooth ride that swoops through turns at over fifty-one mph.

Kings Island is also famous for its classic wooden coasters such as *The Beast,* which truly lives up to its name. Although it is over twenty years old, it is still the longest wooden roller coaster in the country. It is a ride best enjoyed after dark, truly in a class by itself as it twists and turns through the woods, with a spiral into a long tunnel that will leave you wanting more. Although it is very safe, the aged-looking wood gives you the uneasy feeling that the whole structure could collapse underneath you at any moment, something that adds to your enjoyment of the ride.

If that isn't enough, then you can ride the newest wood coaster to hit the park, the *Son of Beast,* the only looping wood coaster in the world with a 214-foot hill and speeds in excess of sixty mph. Kings Island also has a log flume ride which is a relaxing, cooling way to ride through the treetops, ending with a splash that will feel great on a hot day! And if you like drop rides, then head to the *Drop Zone* and feel your heart drop when you plunge twenty-six stories from a height of 315 feet straight down, at speeds that

Pete Trabucco

surpass sixty mph. This is, at the time of this writing, the tallest gyro drop in the world!

Overall at Kings Island, there is plenty of fun to be had for the whole family. The shows are very entertaining, and there are lots of attractions (rides and shows) for smaller kids in the two major kids' areas of the park, Hanna-Barbera Land and Nickelodeon Central. And if you can make it till closing time, you'll get to see a great fireworks display to boot. In addition to this, there is a huge water park that in and of itself can be a day's worth of entertainment for the family. At Kings Island, as in other amusement parks, expect long lines at most e-ticket attractions and the usual fast food places, but all in all, it is truly worth the trip.

15 *SeaWorld* in Orlando, Florida may not have many roller coasters or major flume rides, but to me it stands out as one of the best parks around. Sure, I also like SeaWorld in San Diego and SeaWorld in San Antonio, but the one in beautiful Orlando has risen above the rest with the invention of just one ride: *Kraken. Kraken* is a floorless coaster that will give you an experience like no other of its kind. Hanging from the top of the lift hill, you get a bird's eye view of the park, and what a view it is, or if flume rides are your passion, get set for a *Journey to Atlantis,* which is the best of its kind in the nation.

But these two thrill rides are just part of this park's vast popularity. I know I like to talk about coasters, but this park doesn't need them to be successful. Like its counterpart at Busch Gardens in Tampa, it is very educational for the young and old alike. There are few places where you can pet live stingrays in a petting pool. You can also go to the Key West section of the park and touch a dolphin, or feed many different types of fish and mammals. And of course there is the killer whale, Shamu, to entertain the family! Whether you are six or sixty, you will leave the killer whale show greatly impressed with these wondrous and amazing whales. They and their excellent professional trainers put on a show that is simply mesmerizing. Viewers get to see a fun and fanciful side to these massive and majestic creatures.

Terrors of the Deep will give you a close look at the animals that horror films are made from. Among the sharks, barracudas, moray eels, and lionfish, there are many creepy creatures to thrill even the most steadfast visitors. The glass tunnel beneath the tank allows visitors to watch these creatures in their natural habitats.

Then there is the 3D *Wild Arctic* ride, and of course the great SeaWorld tower where you get a 360-degree view of the entire park from over three hundred feet above the park. I have found the blue of the aquariums and the park lake to be breathtaking from these heights. I am pretty sure you will too.

And, as of 2003, is the waterfront at SeaWorld, a place where you can unwind and celebrate the sights, sounds (as well as food), and festivity of this vibrant city by the sea. Overall, there is so much to see and do at this park that it definitely makes my top twenty-five list.

16

Six Flags America in Largo, Maryland is a great park for those who like a little bit of everything. Located just fifteen minutes outside of Washington, D.C., Six Flags America started out primarily as a water park called Wild World in the '70 s. The Adventure World name changed the park's focus away from water rides to a more traditional amusement park genre that is currently in operation. With the Six Flags changeover in 1999, it became the amusement park that we all see today, a modern-day, competitive amusement park chock full of popular Six Flags Warner Brothers characters. Six Flags America features more than one hundred thrilling rides, shows, and attractions, headlined by eight fun and furious roller coasters! It is the home of the legendary coaster *Superman— Ride of Steel,* at two hundred feet one of the tallest and fastest hypercoasters in the world. If you feel the need to fly like a bird, there is always *Batwing,* the incredible inverted coaster that literally has to be experienced to be believed.

Let's not forget the other great coasters this park

has as well. They are the wooden coaster *Roar* and the *Wild One*, as well as great steel coasters like *Jokers Jinx*, *Mind Eraser* and *Two Face, the Flip Side*. For the kids, there are Bugs Bunny and all the Looney Toons at, where else, Looney Toons Movie Town. The park also features live Hollywood-style shows, plus a huge water park called Paradise Island. (The "island" is filled with more than a million gallons of splashin' action.)

Guests of all ages can enjoy the sensational rides, games, shows and attractions, and *recently* Six Flags America has *added* a cool new water ride. *The Penguin's Blizzard River,* the tallest spinning rapids ride (over sixty feet) in the world is the first to feature the popular Batman theme, based on the legendary DC Comics *Super Heroes* and Batman's arch-nemesis, The Penguin. It looks good! You will find this to be a really enjoyable water park.

The other thing I really like about this park is the parking. There really isn't a bad parking spot in the complex. No need for trams or trains to move you where the action is. All in all it is a great park, a little on the small side as Six Flag parks go, but still well worth the admission price.

17 *Six Flags Great Adventure* in Jackson, New Jersey is one of the best parks in the nation. Sure, I am a little prejudiced about it, since I live just twenty minutes away from this park. But I say, "If you are going to have a park right in your backyard, there are only a few others in the country that are better than this one." Originally built by Warner Leroy, the park received its trademark name of Great Adventure. In 1977 the park became part of the Six Flags chain, and today over three and a half million people visit the park every year. Situated on 120 acres of land and boasting thirteen roller coasters, Six Flags Great Adventure is a destination park for just about everyone, especially if you are a roller coaster fanatic. If you truly want to be tested on your thrill factor, very few parks surpass the coasters you will find here. First, there is the floorless marvel *Medusa*, then *Batman and Robin-the Chiller*, the infamous *Batman the Ride* and of course the huge 230-foot wonder *Nitro*. Also, if you prefer wood coasters, *Rolling Thunder* (my personal favorite) is still there and running as well as ever and let's not forget *El Toro!*

Boasting more rides and attractions than any other park in the country, Six Flags Great Adventure has recently added twenty-five new rides and attractions. One such ride is the new flying coaster *Superman the Escape,* a ride that allows you to fly like a bird underneath the tracks with nothing between you and the ground but a harness. Now that's sweet! You also have not one, but two kiddy sections to this park. There's Loony Toons seaport and an unfortunately ever-shrinking Bugs Bunny land. You can also find the park's trademark two hundred-foot parachute perch and a float down a pretty decent river rapids ride in *Conga River Rapids.* Plus, if you like animals, right next door is the Six Flags Wild Safari, the world's largest drive-thru safari outside of Africa. This 350-acre wildlife preserve stretches four point five miles and features eleven themed sections with nearly 1200 animals. This is the place to go in the tri-state area (New York/New Jersey/Pennsylvania) if you are truly looking for a Great Adventure on the east coast.

18 *Six Flags Great Escape* is nestled in the foothills of the Adirondack Mountains located in Lake George, New York. The Great Escape has gone under many different names since its inception in 1954, but I found this park to be one of the nicest places, especially if you want to get away from the city. Situated right next to Lake George, this park boasts the area's best thrill rides and roller coasters, plus delicious food, games, and all the fun and excitement you can handle. There are seven roller coasters here, and if you like wooden coasters, one of the best can be found in this park. *The Comet* at Six Flags Great Escape Fun Park is, in a word, Fantastic! A former nationally top-ranked wooden coaster, *Comet* continues to exhibit the attributes that made it famous. Not too long ago, if you were looking for the best wooden coaster in the country, you had to come here to find it.

Great Escape also boasts five other coasters you

will surely enjoy. New is *Canyon Blaster.* Originally at Opryland USA in Nashville, Tennessee, *The Canyon Blaster* in the Ghost Town section of the park is an outstanding family mine train ride, which dovetails nicely with the reputation of this family-style park. With two lift hills, a top speed of forty-five miles per hour, and a thrilling double helix, this ride is just great for the whole family. *Canyon Blaster* is just the latest in a string of improvements and innovative new rides that have been added at The Great Escape since Six Flags, Inc. purchased the park in 1996.

Among the additions are three roller coasters—the *Nightmare at Crack Axle Canyon,* the *Alpine Bobsled* (originally at Six Flags Great Adventure), and the *Boomerang Coaster.* Other additions to the park have been the *Skycoaster, Lumberjack Splash* wave pool at Splashwater Kingdom, *Paul Bunyan's Bucket Brigade,* and an Olympiad-style grand prix go-cart track. This might not be one of the best parks in the thrill ride department, but when you add the beautiful lake, the majestic mountains, the nice people, and a great family atmosphere, location means just about everything. Add to these the great shows that this park puts together every year, and you might just want to add this one to your list.

19 *Six Flags Magic Mountain* in Valencia, California is another one of the e-ticket mega parks that is a must for all those who want to experience extreme rides. Just outside of Los Angeles, the *Mountain* is billed not just as a theme park but quite rightly as an "Xtreme park." Recently it has unveiled its sixteenth coaster, created by coaster design experts Bolliger & Mabillard of Switzerland. *Scream* is the only ride of its kind in southern California. Since the park's inception in 1971, Six Flags Magic Mountain continues to deliver the next generation of thrill rides, and with *Scream* the park now ties Cedar Point in total coasters offered to the public and in fact directly competes with the Point as the top place to go to be thrilled. In 2002, prior to *Scream,* the park introduced *X2,* the most anticipated ride of the decade, and *Déjà Vu,* the tallest and fastest suspended, looping coaster in the world.

Also in the record books is another coaster worth mentioning, *Superman the Escape,* the first ride to break the one hundred mph speed barrier. You can find *Viper* at Magic Mountain as well, the tallest looping coaster in the world. *Colossus* was at one time the tallest wooden coaster on the west coast. For those who don't want to remain seated during a ride, the *Riddler's Revenge* is the tallest and fastest stand-up coaster on the planet. And of course there is the steel legend, *Revolution,* the coaster that was the world's first 360-degree looping coaster and was highlighted in the blockbuster movie *Roller Coaster.*

With all these coasters available, Magic Mountain also offers a *fast lane* premium pass program. With this pass, you can ride the best attractions when you want and reduce your wait dramatically! *Fast lane* is a relatively new line management system that (for a fee) allows a limited number of guests the opportunity to all but eliminate the lines associated with Six Flags' most popular attractions! Like all Six Flags parks, its shows are also entertaining, the food is okay, and it has many rides for the kids and younger adults in the family.

20 *Six Flags New England*, located just over the Connecticut border in Agawam, Massachusetts, has changed its reputation quickly since Six Flags took over the reins in 1999. Keeping up the reputation of other Six Flags parks, the new management really cleaned up the place a lot. Rides were painted over, litter seems to be less noticeable, and the park simply grew in name and stature. Changes also came from some new attractions.

One such attraction has made this truly a destination park. The coaster that was selected for this transformation was the third version of an already established legend, but this one literally broke the mold, offering more airtime, steep drops and speed than the vast majority of roller coasters worldwide. I am talking about *Superman—Ride of Steel,* the ride which has literally put this park on the map. Since then, newer rides like *Batman Dark Knight, Night Wing,* and of course *Superman—Ride of Steel* have continued to make this a destination park and one that the whole family will enjoy.

Like all Six Flags parks, this park offers the *fast lane* service, which is very much like the fast pass concept you find at all Disney parks. The *fast lane* allows you to get a ticket for one of the main attractions at Six Flags, so you don't have to wait in line. Like Disney parks, you come back at a certain time and just get on the ride. Unfortunately, unlike Disney, this privilege will cost you a little bit extra.

Overall, you will find more than 150 rides, shows, and attractions here, which make it the largest family theme park in New England. This sixty-five-acre theme park offers eight roller coasters and a two hundred-foot tower for you to be dropped down or shot up. It's your choice! Also, you will find a nice water park, *Island Kingdom,* for kids as well as adults, with a nice wave pool to boot. It might not be the biggest park on my list but overall, it truly offers a lot of excitement for the kid in all of you.

21

Six Flags Over Texas was the first park ever created for the Six Flags chain and is located in Arlington, Texas, a small city between Dallas and Ft. Worth. From its humble beginnings, it has developed into one of the premier amusement parks in the country. It all started in 1961 when Texas oil baron Angus Wynne pioneered the regional theme park industry with the opening of Six Flags Over Texas. Wynne built a broad entertainment product close to where people lived, making it convenient and affordable. He got the idea to name his park from a little Texas history. It seems that six national flags have flown over Texas since the first European exploration of the region by Cortez, which took place in 1519. These countries consisted of Spain, France, Mexico, Texas as a lone republic, Texas within the confederacy, and Texas as a state in the United States. Thus the name of the park was created.

Six Flags Over Texas elevated the old amusement park concept to a true theme park experience with ingenious use of themed presentations, innovative rides and action-packed shows geared to entertain the entire family. I found this park to be a real winner. You will find a slew of great roller coasters, themed rides and special shows here, and it is well worth the admission price to get in. From the down-home country folk that man the rides, to the first-rate entertainment, it is top-class. The best view of the park can be found on the *Oil Derrick*, a three hundred-foot observation platform. Today the park boasts eleven top coasters, including the 255-foot steel marvel *Titan* and, of course, the notorious wooden legend, the *Texas Giant*.

From this one park grew Six Flags, Inc., a company well known for the hottest coasters, thrill rides, and shows around the world. Six Flags, Inc. is currently the world's largest regional theme park company, with a total of thirty-seven parks throughout the United States, Europe, and Latin America.

22 *Universal Studios Florida/ and California*. Universal Studios in Orlando, Florida is all about Hollywood and the film industry, with more big-ticket rides and more activities than Disney's Hollywood Studios but less moviemaking lore. Universal Florida is larger than its counterpart in California (and does not have the second park–Universal Studio's, Island of Adventure but both parks offer the visitor an inside look at how moviemaking is done. The park's key attractions are the thrill rides—like the new *The Simpsons Ride, Terminator 2: 3-D* (a 3-D movie with live action stunts) and *The Revenge of the Mummy* (which is my personal favorite), a roller coaster that hurdles you through darkness both backward and forward. Also very popular is *Jimmy Neutron's Nicktoon Blast*, based on the Nickelodeon cartoon, where you board a rocking and rolling spaceship and follow Jimmy into space. There you meet a variety of Nickelodeon characters, including SpongeBob SquarePants and the Rugrats. Capitalizing on the success of Shrek is Shrek 4-D, a 3-D movie that adds sensory touches to a continuation of the film as Lord Farquaad attempts to do away with the ogre, his bride and donkey.

Finally, if you like creepy, then you should visit the creepy comedy at Fear Factor Live. Also, the classic rides are also there. Rides like *Jaws, Twister* and *Earthquake* are essentially variations on the same theme: You can also find tamer attractions for small children include a ride with E.T which is a must see-must experience event in the park. Indeed, there is a lot to do in this park and expect to be in the park several days to experience it all. If you like horror, you will love the Universal Horror Make-up Show. Try and seat yourself up-front so you really get a great view of all the make-up and blood making tricks used in movies scariest scenes. They call on volunteers to help them with this show and it is one the kids all love. If you like magic and horror together, you will really love this show!

One note to make regarding getting past those long lines at Universal. In Florida, if you are staying at any of the Universal Resorts; Portofino Bay Hotel, the Hard Rock Café Hotel, or The Royal Pacific Resort, you can get in (most times) without even waiting just by showing you hotel key. At these hotels, you can most likely knock off Universal Studios in a day and a half and Islands of Adventure in about the same time period.

23 *Universal Studio's Islands of Adventure*, located in Orlando, Florida is one of the newest parks (built in 1999) in the area and easily makes my list of top parks for several reasons. If you are a coaster fanatic, this park holds two of the sweetest coasters in the world, three if you count *Dueling Dragons'* twin track experience. One of the best coasters in the world, most surveys agree, is Islands of Adventure's *Incredible Hulk.* And Islands of Adventure doesn't stop there. If you love water rides, you have a few options in this park. From *Dudley Do-right's Ripsaw Falls* to the eighty-five-foot drop at Jurassic Park's *River Adventure,* or *Popeye and Bluto's Bilge Rat Barges,* it is a sure thing that you are going to get wet. If you like heights and being shot up a 220-foot tower at speeds reaching forty-nine miles per hour, then *Dr. Doom's Fearfall* is the ride for you. If 3-D is your thing, then you can experience the best simulated dark ride around; *Spiderman's* 3-D experience will make you feel like you are right in the middle of the action.

Overall you get five "Islands" to choose from:

Toon Lagoon, Marvel Super Hero Island, Jurassic Park, the Lost Continent, and Seuss Land for the kids. If you visit the park around Christmastime, do not miss the special Grinch show shown in three parts at Seuss Land. You will truly enjoy it. There is literally something for everyone in this park and it is well worth the price of admission.

Like at Disney, you will find some of the best hotels right at the park. They are the Portofino Bay Hotel, the Hard Rock Café Hotel, and Universal's newest hotel, the Royal Pacific Resort. Right next door you have Islands of Adventure's sister park, Universal Studios, Florida. And if that isn't enough, and if rides, shows and attractions don't really interest you, fear not, there is always City Walk for your shopping, dining, and live entertainment pleasure. They are so popular that both parks combined cater to almost thirteen million people a year (five and a half for Islands of Adventure and seven plus million at Universal Studios, Florida). These parks have it all, and I could literally write a book about all there is to do here. Oops, that was already done by someone else!

24 *Walt Disney World* in Orlando, Florida is in my mind still one of top places to go on a vacation. Does it have the most thrilling roller coasters around? Well, no. Does it have the best live shows for adults? Well, not really, but what it does have can only be described as pure magic to your senses! Talk all you want about other parks. You still have to give Disney World the highest marks for concept, theming, and overall presentation. As you all know, Disney World is comprised of many different parks. First there is the Magic Kingdom, home of Mickey and crew, with 1001 things to do that will surely keep your four-to-ten year old totally mesmerized. For the adults you can't beat *Splash Mountain* or roller coaster favorites like *Space Mountain* and the *Runaway Train*. Children also have their own coaster in *Goofy's Barnstormer* located in Toon Town.

Then there is *Animal Kingdom*, home of *Dinosaur*, *A Bug's Life* and *Primeval Whirl* just to name a few. The shows here are also very good. *The Lion King* and *The Little Mermaid* stand out as better than average, and your kids will also love the hundreds

Pete Trabucco

of animals in the park. *Animal Kingdom* is very educational and an interesting departure from most other theme parks.

Another feature is Disney's MGM Hollywood Studios, the home of the *Tower of Terror*, in my mind, still one of the best drop rides around. For the roller coaster enthusiast there is *Rock-n-Roller Coaster*, a souped-up version of *Space Mountain* that really is worth riding. Again, there are hundreds of rides, shows and attractions that really make your trip to MGM Hollywood Studios worthwhile.

Finally there is *EPCOT*, a little light on thrill rides, except for *Test Track*, but still an adventure for everyone. You might not know this, but at its inception, Epcott was labeled as the city of the future and Walt Disney's dream of what the modern world would look like in the new millennium. We now know that his vision in the '70 s was not quite on track, but you will have a hard time hearing me complain about this masterpiece of a park. Nations literally come together in celebration of cultures and societies, all within walking distance. All in all, these four Disney parks are truly beautiful and absolutely amazing in their own unique ways, with rides and attractions for just about everyone. They are set up for those of you who truly want to discover the child in you and to experience the sheer joy in your little ones' eyes. One thing for sure, make sure you get a park-hopper pass so you can go between parks and stay on Disney property if you can. The friendly staff and above-average service are the best there is. While you're there, you should also visit the downtown Disney area, the boardwalk, and the *Typhoon Lagoon* and *Blizzard Beach* water parks. Many books have been written about this magical theme park monopoly, as well they should. My review here is simply created to entice you to book a trip as soon as possible. You and your family will be happy you did.

25 *Canada's Wonderland* Park is one of the best-attended seasonal theme parks in North America and annually over 3 million visitors visit this Canadian roller coaster Mecca. This combination theme park and water park is located minutes north of Toronto. At 330-acres, Canada's Wonderland is the largest theme park in Canada and offers more than 200 attractions, including an impressive lineup of 60 amusement rides. It is here that you will find Behemoth, the 15th roller coaster at Canada's Wonderland and this B&M monstrosity is quite impressive. At 230 feet high, it is the tallest roller coaster in Canada. Overall, Canada's Wonderland boasts 15 thrilling roller coasters and the largest selection of flat rides for any park in the world. The adjoining 20-acre Splash Works Waterpark is included with park admission and offers 16 water slides, a lazy river and the largest wave pool in Canada. Canada's Wonderland theme park is owned and operated by Cedar Fair Entertainment based in Sandusky, Ohio. Canada's Wonderland opened on May 23, 1981 after two years of construction. The park was eventually purchased by Viacom and re-branded Paramount Canada's Wonderland. In June 2006, Viacom sold the Paramount Parks chain to Sandusky, Ohio based park operator Cedar Fair and a year later the Paramount name was dropped reverting back to the original name, Canada's Wonderland. If you are ever in the Toronto area, this amusement park is a classic and one that offers a little something for everyone. I am quite sure you will like it...

Pete Trabucco

The Top 25 Coasters from the Birthplace of
the Modern-Day Roller Coaster

New York, New Jersey, and Connecticut not only are known for having the best beaches around, they are also home to many different amusement parks and some of the very best roller coasters in the country. If you're looking to visit some of the best parks around the nation, then you need look no further than the parks in the tri-state area. One of the best overall parks in the area is Six Flags Great Adventure in Jackson, New Jersey, but along with it come many others. If you're looking for the best wooden coaster around, look no further than Astroland Amusement Park, home of the Coney Island *Cyclone,* in Brooklyn, New York.

Also, if you want to combine the Jersey Shore with thrill rides, then you can head to one of several boardwalk amusement parks located on the beach. You will surely find coaster excitement and wet rides at Morey's Piers in Wildwood, as well as many more rides and attractions in Seaside, Atlantic City; and Ocean City, New Jersey. And if you are looking for one of the best wooden coasters ever built, drive north to Lake Compounce in Bristol, Connecticut and experience *Boulder Dash,* the best wood coaster in the east! Overall, you can find something for everyone at any of the eighteen amusement parks that the tri-state area, especially New Jersey, has to offer.

Here are my Top 25 Coasters
from the Birthplace of the Modern-day Roller Coaster

I.   *Nitro* at Six Flags Great Adventure in Jackson, New Jersey.

2. *Kingda Ka* at Six Flags Great Adventure in Jackson, New Jersey

3. *Medusa* at Six Flags Great Adventure in Jackson, New Jersey.

4. *Boulder Dash* at Lake Compounce in Bristol, Connecticut.

5. *El Toro* at Six Flags Great Adventure in Jackson, New Jersey.

6. *Great White* at Morey's Pier in Wildwood, New Jersey.

7. *The Cyclone* at Coney Island in Brooklyn, New York.

8. *Superman—(The Flying Coaster)*, Six Flags Great Adventure.

9. *Batman—The Dark Knight*, Six Flags Great Adventure.

10. *Batman the Ride (Inverted BTR)* at Six Flags Great Adventure.

11. *The Comet* at Six Flags Great Escape in Lake George, New York.

12. *The Sea Serpent (Boomerang) coaster* at Morey's Pier in Wildwood.

13. *The Great Nor'Easter (SLC)* at Morey's Pier in Wildwood.

14. *The Great American Scream Machine* at Six Flags Great Adventure.

15. *Rolling Thunder* at Six Flags Great Adventure.

16. *The Dragon Coaster* at Rye Playland in Rye, New York.

17. *Skull Mountain* at Six Flags Great Adventure.

18. *The Jack Rabbit Coaster* at Clementon Park.

19. *The Crazy Mouse (Spinning Coaster)* at Steel Pier in Atlantic City.

20. *The Python (Zyclon Loop)* at Playland in Ocean City.

21. *The Runaway Train (Mine Train)* at Six Flags Great Adventure.

Pete Trabucco

22. *The Wildcat Coaster* at Keansburg Amusement Park.

23. *Roller Coaster* at Funtown Pier in Seaside Heights.

24. *The Doo Wopper (Wild Mouse) Coaster* at Morey's Pier in Wildwood.

25. *Blackbeard's Lost Treasure Train* at Six Flags Great Adventure in Jackson.

1 *Nitro* at Six Flags Great Adventure in Jackson, New Jersey is without a doubt one of the most intense rides that I have ever had the privilege of riding. From its 215-foot (the tallest B&M coaster to date), sixty-six-degree drop to the high-g turnaround section, it is a wild ride that you will not soon forget. Bolliger and Mabillard (B&M) do it again with this one, which is currently ranked fifth in the world for steel coasters by *Amusement Today* magazine. It is safe to say that *Nitro* is more than just your "average" hypercoaster. It's an elite machine among elite machine coasters. And even

though its L-shaped out and back layout borrows plenty from *Apollo's Chariot* in Williamsburg, Virginia (another favorite coaster of mine), this monster definitely has some new tricks up its sleeve. At this steep drop, the angle of the first decent looks absolutely vertical. from this dizzying height, it sure feels like you are diving straight down the tracks. In addition to the eye-opening first drop, *Nitro* has plenty of secondary drops, turns, and high-speed maneuvers that will literally keep you guessing and out of breath. No matter how many times you ride this coaster, a different element will shock and amaze you. The best seat on this ride is in the first row, left front. The reason for this occurs on the ride's second drop. A 189-foot plunge to the left leaves the unsuspecting passenger stationed in that seat helplessly looking straight down at the ground below. Racing at speeds in excess of eighty mph, this ride has seven steep drops, two highly banked horizontal loops, and an eye-opening hammerhead semi-loop element that is sure to wake you up. On the way up the lift hill, riders will notice signs which point out how high they are in comparison to famous structures, such as the Sphinx in Egypt (sixty-six feet), Niagara Falls (176 feet), and the Statue of Liberty (189 feet). Overall, the ride is extremely smooth and is completely airtime-filled. Clearly the best and most intense ride at Great Adventure, but watch out for those lines. They can be pretty long at times. Not recommended for the faint of heart, this one is a ride from which you build up high g negative and positive tolerances.

2 *Kingda Ka* at Six Flags Great Adventure in Jackson, New Jersey is not just the biggest and fastest coaster in the world...it's also the baddest! Kingda Ka, the newest ride at Six Flags, stands more than forty-five stories tall at 456 feet—roughly three times the height of the Statue of Liberty—and propels riders at speeds of approximately 130 mph in less than four seconds. This is more than fifty-five mph faster than the *Batman and Robin* roller coaster and forty-five mph faster than the beloved *Nitro* also located at the Jackson, New Jersey park. In addition, the ride's fall is performed at a 270-degree angle spiral, corkscrewing riders as they descend at record-breaking speeds. When *Kingda Ka* opened in 2005, the coaster broke all the records. What if a coaster could be launched at 128 miles per hour in just a few seconds, be catapulted to the dizzying height of 450 feet, plummet down at 120 mph and still be back to the starting gate in less than 30 seconds. Well the manufacturer (B&M) came up a ride that would do all of these things and much more. *Kinda Ka* is very similar to another powerhouse ride called *Top Thrill Dragster* but unlike *Top Thrill,* you never know when you are going to be rocketed down the 3,118-foot long track and at the end of *Kingda Ka;* get ready for a 130 foot hill that will literally pull you out of your seat. At the top of this last hill, you will experience zero gravity and know what it feels like to be in outer space if only for a second or two. All in all, *Kingda Ka* is an experience you must not miss and make sure you wear some eye protection. At these speeds you will need it.

3 *Medusa* at Six Flags Great Adventure is a treasure to behold! Have you ever wanted to be strapped in a chair with your feet dangling

Pete Trabucco

precariously while you were fourteen stories high? Better yet, have you ever been strapped to a chair whose sole purpose is to fly through a powerful series of twists, turns, and looping inversions at speeds that reach over sixty mph? If you've answered yes to both of these questions, then chances are, you've experienced the unique, exhilarating, unforgettable thrill ride from the new generation of manmade adrenaline machines. More than likely, you experienced it on a ride created by Bolliger and Mabillard (B&M) known as the first "floorless" roller coaster ever to be created. *Medusa* went into the history books on April 2, 1999, when it streaked down the tracks as the nation's *first* floorless roller coaster. This 140-foot monster gives you a great view of the drive-through safari (but only for a split second) before you plummet at speeds reaching in excess of sixty miles per hour. Also, since the track is below you and your feet dangle just inches from it, you might want to look anywhere else but down at your feet as you speed across the course. There is a great feet-chopping effect all through this ride, just one of the interesting things about floorless coasters. They make you want to have the shortest legs possible. *Nitro* is also packed with incredible oversized fun and has seven thrill-packed inversions that are guaranteed to put a smile on your face, including a vertical loop, dive loop, the zero-g roll (the best), cobra roll (two inversions), and two corkscrews. This one is truly a winner and is highly recommended for those coaster enthusiasts who would like to experience the best the industry has to offer.

4 *Boulder Dash* at Lake Compounce in Bristol, Connecticut is in my mind one of the very best, wooden coasters ever created. Upon boarding one of the two spacious Philadelphia Toboggan Company trains, your journey begins with a serene and picturesque trip up the lift hill. Cresting into a scenic ninety-degree turn, riders are given just enough time to relax before the drop and a ride you will not soon forget! This coaster has it all. At 4500-feet long, *Boulder Dash* is to date the *only* coaster that literally was built along the side of a mountain.

It is one of the largest and fastest wood coasters I have ridden to date. At 155-feet high and reaching speeds of sixty mph, all the pieces come together in a presentation that constantly gives you a fun-filled thrill ride experience. It is a smooth and great family coaster, set up in one of the most family-oriented amusement parks I have been to. I consistently get off this ride feeling like I got really my money's worth. The trick I think is that since most of the course is wooded, you never do know what's up ahead. The ride literally dashes through trees and around rocks, and unlike most wooden coasters has a consistent ride throughout. The majestic mountain setting also makes this ride a one-of-a-kind experience. Ranked by *Amusement Today* as one of the top five best coasters on the planet (and after riding it, I can see why) there really isn't a bad seat anywhere. I will tell you that I prefer the front row on this one. A great ride for everyone this is a coaster well worth waiting in line for, and the best news is that there are very rarely long lines at this top attraction.

5 *El Toro* at Six Flags Great Adventure in Jackson, New Jersey is one of the best wooden roller coasters in the Northeast! Riding *El Toro* is something any coaster enthusiast, should put on their list of coasters to conquer. With one of the steepest drops (seventy-six degrees) on the planet and the feeling of full speed ahead throughout the ride, *El Toro* is unmatched for its tenacity and re-ridability. The fast lift hill reminiscent of *Millennium Force* keeps you guessing on what will be next. The placement of this ride is also something to marvel at. The *El Carnival* section is appropriately themed with a Spanish flare. Situated where the *Old Viper* coaster was, the ride fits perfectly into the area and delivers more thrills than most other Six Flags rides combined at the park. The trains are themed somewhat like mine train cars and have a very comfortable, next generation look and feel. Loading the trains is a bit slow, but the trains are longer than normal holding thirty-six riders compared to twenty-four on *Thunderhead* and the twenty-eight stowed on *The Voyage*. The height of *El Toro* (176

Pete Trabucco

feet) may not be the tallest around but that first drop is a memorable one, and I have to say one of the best first drops that I have experienced on a wooden coaster. The overall out and back (with a twist) coaster reminded me a lot of *Shivering Timbers* at Michigan Adventure but with a lot more pop in the saddle. What I found most interesting even though this is a very intense ride, is how smooth it was throughout. You would think you were riding a steel coaster (like *Nitro*) but you are on wood. The airtime of *El Toro* is sensational and *Intamin's Prefabricated Wooden Coaster* in my mind really delivers a real bang for the buck. This is the type of coaster you seek out, and along with *Nitro* and *Kingda Ka* are the sole reasons why you come to this Six Flags Park.

6 *Great White* at Morey's Pier in Wildwood, New Jersey is a must for all wooden coaster lovers to ride. One of the two things I most enjoy (and so will you) about *Great White* are that at 110 feet, the top of the lift hill gives you an absolutely amazing view of the Atlantic Ocean. The second thing I love about this ride is that after you complete the fifty mile per hour first drop, you will literally feel as though your body is being ejected out of your seat and into the ocean as you enter the turnaround element that directly overlooks the beach area. All through the ride, there are amazing drops and high-speed turns and twists that make this 3300-foot marvel very popular among roller coaster enthusiasts. During the ride you will also pass quite close to a nearby skyride (a good place to check out *Great White*) and speed down the track while an ocean breeze blasts you straight in the face. The negative-g drops experienced on this ride are just phenomenal. Also on *Great White*, just after you leave the station, you will literally go through the floor of the pier itself and under it before you start your climb to the top of the first lift hill. This combination twister and double-out destination coaster is a top attraction, and since this is a pay-as-you-go park, it is one coaster that you can ride over and over for mere peanuts. It is definitely worth the trip to the Jersey shore.

7 *The Cyclone* at Astroland Park in Coney Island is still the wooden coaster that has set the standard for all others in the nation. Created in 1927 for a mere $175,000, this coaster still ranks in the top fifteen worldwide, even today, and still packs a wild punch for all those who are lured to it. Located just feet away from the beach, riders get a fantastic view from its eighty-five-foot lift hill before they plunge at sixty miles per hour down one of the steepest first drops, fifty-eight degrees, ever created for a wooden coaster. The *Cyclone* is, in a word, "a classic." From the old style, original bench seats and lap bars to its constant drops, turns and twists, when you ride this coaster, you know you have ridden one of the best in the world! This coaster never seems to slow down through its 3500-foot course, and the ten drops just seem to keep on coming. Since the coaster footprint is small, the g's (both positive and negative) are pretty intense. Famous aviation legend Charles Lindbergh once said that this coaster was "even scarier then flying." If you sit in the very back seat of this contraption, I believe he may have been right. There is also the 1948 story of Emilio Franco, who had an ailment that made it impossible to speak. After a ride on the *Cyclone* he was reported to have spoken his first words, "I feel sick!" The *Cyclone* is one ride that all roller coaster enthusiasts must experience at least once in their lives. It still runs as it did when built and has not been modified to tame it, as many other coasters have. One more thing, after the ride on this Coney Island attraction, you don't even have to leave your seat in order to ride again. Just pay the man as he walks on by and prepare for another sensational ride. Now you just can't beat that!

8 *Superman—Ultimate Flight* at Six Flags Great Adventure is like nothing you have ever ridden. *Superman* is only the second B&M coaster in the world where you can literally *fly* around the track. This coaster offers the rider a sense of flight that can really be intoxicating. On this ride you swoop, dive, and race over the treetops with nothing but an inverted open-air car tethering you. Indeed, it was built upon the idea of taking this coaster to the next level. Flying coasters use an ingenious track layout and a unique coaster car design to replicate the sensation of flight. With special harnesses, there is literally nothing but air separating you and the ground below. It is an odd, but interesting, sensation to hang upside down for what seems to be a long period of time. (The ride itself is only about 140 seconds long.) The inversions on most coasters briefly turn riders upside down, but *Superman* maintains a down position for a large portion of the ride. At first, the urge is to hang on for dear life. (I know I did that.) However, as the ride progresses, you realize that you can trust the harnesses, stretch out your arms and well—fly like Superman through the corkscrews and additional elements on this ride. Packed with five inversions, the ride literally flies you through the course at almost fifty-five miles per hour. Also on the ride, make note that during the top of the pretzel loop, you enter this element on your back and then fly through the loop in a forward position, making it a sensational one-of-a-kind ride experience.

9 *The Dark Knight Coaster* located at Six Flags Great Adventure in Jackson, New Jersey. More than just a mouse ride, *The Dark Knight* coaster features the best world-beloved DC Comics characters (The Batman Crew) in an adventure that utilizes storytelling, physical movement, video, sound, and special effects to bring guests a one-of-a-kind dark ride thrill. As part of the experience, park guests will see, hear, and feel the action of the movie the moment they enter the ride queue line, as they are transformed into citizens of Gotham City—caught in the middle of a city under siege and torn apart by The Joker. Riders board a special car and fly through several elements that include drops in the dark and neck flinchig 180-degree turns. It is said that the "*The Dark Knight* coaster offers guests a one-of-a-kind ride experience that combines the action and excitement of The Dark Knight movie with the thrill of a roller coaster," said Mark Kane,

Six Flags Great Adventure's Park President. The $7.5 million coaster is located in the Movietown section at Six Flags Great Adventure adjacent to *Batman the Ride*. Guests can receive up-to-the-minute park news and purchase a new season pass online at www.sixflags.com.

10 *Batman the Ride* at Six Flags Great Adventure may be getting old but is still one of the best inverted coasters ever built. True, there are many taller and faster inverted coasters around, but when you experience this ride's intensity, in this case bigger is not always better. Since *Batman* has a small footprint, the g-forces attained going through a particular element are much higher (due to tighter turns on faster track) and can be particularly exhilarating. The ride sustains heavy g-loading (sometimes as high as 5 g's) and maintains a constant speed throughout the course. The best seats for visuals are, of course, the front four, but if you really want to get knocked around (and most of us do), try the four back seats at night. There are very few lights on this attraction in the evening, and if you ride at this time you will have no idea where the heck you are going. Bolliger and Mabillard (B&M) can be very proud of this invention concocted over a decade ago. Also worth mentioning is the queue through Gotham City while you are entering the ride. It is done well and sets the perfect mood for your adventure. If you can't visit New Jersey, you can find this ride at Six Flags Magic Mountain, Six Flags Over Georgia, Six Flags Over Texas, and where the ride originated in 1992 at Six Flags Great America in St. Louis.

11 *The Comet* at Six Flags Great Escape Fun Park in Lake George, New York is, in a word, "Fantastic." A former nationally top-ranked wooden coaster, *Comet* continues to exhibit the attributes which earned it this highest accolade. The *Comet* was first constructed in 1927 by legendary coaster builder Harry Traver. Back then, it was called the *Cyclone*, and it was thought by many to be the most intense coaster at

Batman the Ride at Six Flags Great Adventure

that time. It had a laminated wood track with a steel superstructure but was considered a wooden coaster by definition. At ninety-five feet high and a pretty fair eighty seven-foot drop, *Comet* seems to get faster and wilder as it scours the tracks at over fifty five miles per hour. There is a bunny hop heaven with a double out and back setup, of which the Philadelphia Toboggan Company can be very proud. As you continue through your run, the turns seem to get tighter and tighter, and there are several unexpected and venomous little side twists en route that will take your breath away. The final turnaround is where this coaster really shines. You seem to be again picking up speed as you enter the final turnaround, and you truly feel as if you are about to be ejected from your seat. This ride packs a punch and if you love negative g's, you will truly love this roller coaster. It has been my experience that the lines are never really too long at this park, and most days you will be able to ride again and again to your heart's content. Enjoy!

12 *The Sea Serpent* at Morey's Pier in Wildwood, New Jersey was the first of its type ever to hit America's shores. Created by Vekoma Corporation in 1984, this standard shuttle takes riders backward up to a height of 125 feet. At the top of the station, the train is released and drops through the station into a boomerang or cobra roll element, where it goes through a vertical loop and up a second lift hill. Here the train is pulled forward to the top and then released backward over the same 825-foot course. I think the best part of this or any shuttle-type coaster ride is traversing the course backward, and this one is a real pleaser. It is quite different from the closed-track coaster style and is an experience that all coaster enthusiasts ought to try. While the ride might be a little rough by today's standards, in my opinion it is worth riding. Unfortunately since only one train can be dispatched at a time, the lines tend to get pretty long on busy days. In addition to the *Sea Serpent* are many other notable boomerang coasters around the country you can ride. They are the *Boomerang* at Knott's Berry Farm, Six Flags Fiesta Texas, and Six Flags Great Escape; *Sidewinder* at Hershey Park; *Tidal Wave* at Trimpers Rides; and *Mind Eraser* at Six Flags Worlds of Adventure. You can find three dozen more of these shuttle coasters all over the world, making them the most common large-production model roller coasters ever built.

13 *The Great Nor'Easter* at Morey's Piers in Wildwood, New Jersey may be a standard Vekoma five-inversion roller coaster, but because if its location you get a lot for the money. This coaster is built literally out on the pier, so when you are on the top of the lift hill, the first thing you notice is blue sky, the wind whipping your face, and the ocean all around you. That is, of course, until you begin to dive to the right toward the pier below, reaching speeds of fifty-five miles per hour. You don't always get a smooth ride on the *Great Nor'Easter*. It's like catching the perfect wave, but depending on the day, if you hit it just right, you will get a pretty intense and enjoyable ride.

The *Nor'Easter* seats two abreast in trains that carry the older horse-collar restraints. This ride actually changed a few of its struts and moved the station in order to fit at its present location. It is quite interesting how this coaster wraps itself around the water flume (one of the best on the east coast) and sends riders on their way. The clearances are very tight, and you find yourself raising your legs as much as possible as you ride this SLC (Suspended Looping Coaster), commonly classified as an inverted roller coaster. The SLC possesses five inversions: a cobra roll that inverts the riders twice, a twist loop, and two heartline flips. I consider this ride one of the best of the dozen or so SLC coasters Vekoma has erected in North America. Some of the other Vekoma SLC versions can be found at Six Flags America, Six Flags New England, Six Flags Darien Lake and Six Flags Elitch Gardens. You can also find the coaster under other names, such as *Serial Thriller* at Six Flags Astroworld and Six Flags Worlds of Adventure.

14 *The Great American Scream Machine* at Six Flags Great Adventure was a big deal when it first opened in 1989. Although it is not the e-ticket ride that it used to be, it is still one of the tri-state area's best, and well worth riding. Created by Arrow Dynamics, this coaster was the second of Six Flags' record-breaking trio of looping coasters built in the 1980's. The first was *Shockwave* at Six Flags Great America in Illinois, and the third was *Viper* at Six Flags Magic Mountain in California. All three stand 170 feet tall and speed around the track at around 68 miles per hour *The Scream Machine* is the tallest at 173 feet and has a 155-foot twisting drop to the left, before seven memorable and dizzying inversions. The first loop stands at 136-feet tall, a record for its time, and sets up the rider for the next six ride elements. The old horse-collar restraints might be a little uncomfortable, and the ride can be a head-banger when you compare it to rides with new harnesses, but like its sister coasters is still a good ride. I really enjoy experiencing this coaster at night, when you get a great view of the park itself. *Scream Machine* is now the third-tallest coaster at Great Adventure (behind *Kingda Ka* and *Nitro*), and since the lift hill takes you directly over the park, you can get a great view of Great Adventure's layout while comparing *Scream Machine's* overall height to other award-winning coasters in the park. This is a good coaster for the enthusiast who would like to move up to the next level of intense roller coaster rides.

15 *Rolling Thunder* at Six Flags Great Adventure still holds a very warm place in my heart. You never forget the first real roller coaster you ride, and this one was mine. By today's standards, *Rolling Thunder* is not much to speak of, but even though it was created almost thirty years ago, it still thrills and delights all those who come to ride the *Thunder*. This ninety-six-foot out-and-back wooden coaster races over hills and has dual (separate) tracks. Unlike other coaster racers, its courses are very different, so you actually get two rides in one. Each track was created

Pete Trabucco

The Great American Scream Machine at Six Flags Great Adventure

to offer a distinctive and unique ride experience. I think the right side is tamer than the left and allows the riders to enjoy the view a bit more. However, the left side has clearly the best drops and offers much more airtime for its passengers. One observation I have made about *Rolling Thunder* is that it is one the loudest screeching coasters ever created. The lack of oil on the rails has given *RT* the nickname "*Screeching Thunder*," and after riding it, you will surely know why. On busy days, both trains run simultaneously, and although not as intense as the next-generation wooden racing coasters, they are still a family favorite. The sensation of being lifted out of your seat is quite common on *Rolling Thunder's* left side during the 3200-foot, fifty-five mile per hour course, so if this does not appeal to you, go to the right and directly up the stairs as soon as you enter the queue. The lap bars were old and the paint was peeling everywhere (until in 2003 they finally painted the whole ride) but in my mind, this only makes *Rolling Thunder* more of a classic old-style racer and adds to its overall appeal.

16 *The Dragon Coaster* at Playland Park, Rye, New York, was built in 1929, just after the park debut. It was built by Fred Church and is one of the last remaining examples of his work. This is a very interesting ride with a unique, V-shaped layout. Standing at seventy-five feet tall with a sixty-foot drop, riders fly down the 3400-foot track at speeds reaching in excess of forty-five miles per hour. You notice that this ride seems a little longer than it actually is. This sensation is achieved through its being a multi-layered coaster, and so just when you expect the ride to end, you have another section of track to cover. The *Dragon*, as it is affectionately called, has been featured in many movies, and one of its more memorable moments occurs when you get to go through the dragon's mouth and out through the tail. Kids as well as parents love this ride and it is truly a classic coaster that everyone should experience. Note: Playland Park is a pay-as-you-go park, so you can ride this one many times without notice of any long lines.

Pete Trabucco

17 *Skull Mountain* at Six Flags Great Adventure in Jackson, New Jersey is a good coaster for those who have graduated from the junior coaster ranks and want to try something a little more exciting. Built by Interman and Giovanola in 1986, this indoor coaster has a themed station, and what I really like about it is that riders have to negotiate through a darkened cave-like building in order to get to their destination. When they say "skull mountain," they aren't kidding. The rocky exterior at the front of the building includes a giant skull-like image and dual waterfalls that protrude from the skull's eyes. The ride is also very dark and ominous (unlike Space Mountain at Disney), which adds to the illusion of speed and danger. The actual ride is not very long and its top speed never goes past forty miles per hour. Also, at forty-one feet high, you don't really feel the first forty-seven-foot drop, but you will surely enjoy the tight turns and total darkness which confuses your senses during this 1300-plus foot trek. Since only one train can run at a time, lines can get quite long for this ride, so you might want to allow yourself some time for this one. I enjoyed the front seat for this ride because you can just about make out the track and can see how close you really come to the exterior walls and support beams of the ride itself. It is a pleasant warm-up for the e-ticket rides (*Kingda Ka, Nitro,* and *Medusa*) at this park.

18 *The Jack Rabbit Coaster* at Clemington Park, New Jersey, was built in 1917 and is the second-oldest operational coaster in the country. In fact there is only one coaster in America that can boast to being older (*Leap for Dips* which was created in 1902). Standing at fifty feet high and overlooking most of the park, this ride shoots you down several hills at speeds that reach thirty-eight miles per hour. Created by the legend himself, John Miller, this 1700-foot figure eight design operated with trains with no up-stops, which unfortunately limited the experience quite a bit. However, new trains were added in 1999, and the ride is much better and wilder than it was. It is truly a family coaster and one that the whole family will enjoy. Since trees, foliage, and other rides hide most of the coaster, those who want a preview before they ride it should go on the little park train first to give you a better perspective of the ride itself. But beware! There are elephants, bears, and other wild animals roaming around this area. (You will know that they are not real as you ride by them, by the paint that seems to be peeling off most of them. Still, the kids will enjoy this ride. *The Jack Rabbit* is a fast and enjoyable little woodie, and one that I highly recommend. You kind of get the feeling that, if this ride could talk, oh, the stories it might be able to tell you…

19 *The Crazy Mouse* coaster in Atlantic City was created by Reverchon, taking the wild mouse concept to the next level. Like other wild mouse coasters, this ride ascends a lift hill and is sent down the track, making hairpin turns and negotiating drops that increase as you go along. But there is one major difference: During the second level of the structure, the four-passenger cars spin freely during the ride, instead of always facing forward. This concept spins the cars (like a Virginia wheel) giving the compact, 1377-foot coaster a tremendous and disorienting punch when the cars finally reach the lower level. The *Crazy Mouse* also finds itself in a very special place, located at the famous Steel Pier in Atlantic City. *Crazy Mouse* stands forty-nine feet high with one thirty-foot drop and was the first wild mouse ever to be created in North America. Originally in 1997 this coaster stood at Dinosaur Beach in Wildwood, until it was moved to Atlantic City's famous pier in 1999. The boardwalk hotels add a very special backdrop to this ride and make it an experience to remember. Crazy mouse rides have become very popular in the last few years and can be found at many amusement parks around the world. Some other notable crazy mouse coasters in the United States are *Crazy Mouse* at Motor World in Virginia Beach; *Crazy Mouse* at Myrtle Beach; *Primeval Whirl* at Disney

Pete Trabucco

World's Animal Kingdom, and the *Exterminator* at Kennywood Park.

20 *The Python* at Playland in Ocean City, New Jersey is just one of sixteen zyclon loops created worldwide by Italian-based company Pinfari Corporation. What I like about the *Python* is that you get a good smooth ride from start to finish. It is definitely the ride to choose if you like coasters and want to try adding a loop to your coaster ensemble. Standing at 36-feet high and racing down the 1200-foot long track, this ride will give you a pleasant experience all the way through. Being at the Jersey shore and overlooking the Atlantic Ocean is also a definite plus on any ride, and it is especially a plus for this ride. Usually this type of model has two four-seat cars attached to it, but be careful. The lap bars are pretty snug and, if you are an adult, you might want to hold in your stomach a little to get in. Even though the *Python* has one loop to its credit, this coaster is definitely classified as a family-friendly one, and one that everyone should try. If you are unsure, why not try it and see what happens? If you like this one, then you may be ready for the next level of coaster thrills. This coaster type is actually a progression from other Pinfari non-looping coasters of the same name located all over the world. In fact there are only three of these babies in the United States. You can find the other two under the name of *Looping Star* at the Pier Rides in Ocean City, Maryland; and Beech Bend in Bowling Green, Kentucky.

21 *The Runaway Train* at Six Flags Great Adventure in New Jersey isn't the oldest mine train around (that accolade belongs to the *Mine Train* at Six Flags Over Texas circa 1966), nor is it the tallest or fastest of the two-dozen plus Arrow Corporation mine trains currently in operation. What I can say is that in my opinion, this one is the nicest to ride. Built in 1974 and the first roller coaster to be built at this park, the *Runaway Train* is 2400 feet long (a mine train standard), utilizes one seventy-foot lift hill and races its guests around

Runaway Mine Train at Six Flags Great Adventure (with *Rolling Thunder* in the background)

Pete Trabucco

the track in excess of thirty-five miles per hour. Its scenic views of the park are spectacular, and that last swooping (and most photographed) turn over a manmade lake is a great experience no matter what age you are. I guess this is the one element separating this version from all the rest. Recommended for the advancing beginner coaster aficionado, the *Runaway Train* is indeed a family coaster with a capital "F." In general, mine trains are designed to create the feel of an old runaway boxcar you would find in the Old West. It usually features sharp turns and short little bunny hops. The trains themselves look like coal mining cars, and in most cases you can find mini locomotives (like at Great Adventure) right up front. Except for the tunnels, *Runaway Train* has all these elements. One observation I did make about *Runaway Train* is that if you have small children, it is highly recommended that you make sure your child is a little taller than the minimum height restriction of forty-eight inches. The restraints are old and have a little play in them. I have seen some really small passengers almost eject themselves from

their seats. Please use good judgment here! Other mine trains to look for in America are *Adventure Express* at Paramount's Kings Island; *Cedar Creek Mine Ride* at Cedar Point; *Goldrusher* at Six Flags Magic Mountain; *Thunder Express* at Dollywood; *Traiblazer* at Hershey Park; and Arrow's latest mine train creation, *Canyon Blaster* at Six Flags Great Escape. Mine trains are also being produced by Morgan Manufacturing Company, so currently you will find a renewed effort in building this type of classic coaster.

22 *The Wildcat* coaster at Keansburg Amusement Park in New Jersey is a great ride for beginners as well as experienced coaster enthusiasts. Created by Anton Schwarzkopf, this coaster might only be fifty feet high, but its figure eight design and high visibility seating arrangement (usually just one car that looks like a German-style automobile) make this a decent ride for just about every local amusement park. The cars seem to glide at times as they traverse each end of the 1380-foot structure. But what make the *Wildcat* a classic Schwarzkopf coaster are the three steep drops of over forty feet that will treat the rider to some unexpected negative g's at a pretty high speed approaching forty miles per hour. A welcome surprise for all those who need to feel the rush, the *Wildcat* can be a little rough at times for its smaller passengers, so please make sure they are well-secured before departing the station. Overall, it delivers a good ride experience for its small size. There are three versions of the *Wildcat* that have been produced in the past. This one at Keansburg is the largest of the three versions. Is this a state-of-the-art thrill ride? Of course not, but for its size, it is an A one family coaster with a lot of mileage left on it, and you will find over twenty-five of these coasters worldwide. You can also find the *Wildcat* under the same name at Cedar Point in Sandusky, Ohio; Jolly Roger Amusement Park in Ocean City, Maryland; Martin's Fantasy Island in Grand Island, New York; and William's Grove Park in Mechanicsburg, Pennsylvania. It can also be found under the name of *Die Wildcatz* at Busch Gardens Williamsburg; *Cyclone* at Sandspit Cavendish Beach in Canada; and *Rails* at Valley Fair Park in Shakopee, Minnesota.

23 *Roller Coaster* at Funtown Pier in Seaside, New Jersey is a classic because it is the only one of its kind. Standing fifty feet over the boardwalk, it is the only inversion coaster in America created by Interpark Roller Coaster Company of Italy. Slightly taller and rougher than the Pinfari zyclon loop coaster, this one has one of the best views of the Seaside Pier and the Atlantic Ocean that I have ever seen. You are quite literally over the water when you take that first forty-foot drop, and the loop has remarkable, high positive-g-forces as you enter into it. The 1831-foot-long layout consists of sudden drops and spiraling helixes that at some points come quite close to its structure. More than once I found myself consciously positioning my body in the center of the car to avoid the ride's support structure. Again, this is a good beginner ride for those who wish to

Pete Trabucco

experience inversions. I enjoy this ride and as an added bonus while riding, I can almost smell the knishes, hot dogs, and popcorn that are abundant in this park. During the day, the view from the top is fantastic, but there is nothing like being at the top of this lift hill at night, with the ocean breeze blowing, and listening to invisible waves below you hitting the shoreline. It doesn't get any better than that.

24 *The Doo Wopper* coaster at Morey's Pier in New Jersey is a great little ride for the beginner coaster enthusiast. It also is fun for all those in the family who like tame, controlled coasters with a view. From the top, you can get a picturesque view of the Atlantic Ocean and the boardwalk beneath you. Built by Zamperla in 1998, the *Doo Wopper* can be described as a cute and colorful coaster to ride. I really did appreciate the themes, in that as you go up the lift hill and along the top level of track, you see signs for hot dogs, french fries, and other food products that you would normally find at a hamburger stand. The cars are set up to look like '50s convertible cars. While you are at the top, don't forget to look at the funhouse mirror as you roll past. Even though it is labeled as a wild mouse, at times I compare *Doo Wopper* to a "people mover" as opposed to a wild mouse coaster. Still, there are a few little drops in the middle of the ride, and in some places the car gives the impression that it may fall over the edge. Overall, as wild mice go, it's pretty tame. However, I still found it to be a rather nice ride experience, and if the lines aren't that long, that you should not pass up on. Sometimes less is more.

25 *Blackbeard's Lost Treasure Train* by Zierer (Tivoli) is a junior coaster that the whole family can enjoy. You will find this beauty at Six Flags Great Adventure in Jackson, New Jersey. At twenty-six-feet high, guests are subjected to a twenty-five-foot first drop and several twists and turns on what can only be described as one of the longest coaster trains ever created. This single train has a total of twenty cars (sitting two abreast) for a total of forty riders. *Blackbeard* is so long that the whipping action in the back end of the ride is comparable to that of an intermediate coaster double its size. The ride twists around a compact 1164-foot track at speeds approaching twenty-five miles per hour. In the United States there are ten similar coasters operating at this time. You can ride *Poison Ivy's Tangled Train* at Six Flags New England; *Roadrunner Express* at Six Flags World of Adventure; and *Timber Twister* at Bonfante Gardens in Oregon. Larger custom versions of this ride can also be found at Knott's Berry Farm in California under *Jaguar* and in the indoor Mall of America at Camp Snoopy in Minnesota under the name of the *Pepsi Ripsaw.*

The Future of Coasters—
The Sky Is Literally the Limit!

Well, as you can see, the future of roller coasters looks very promising. Was it just twenty years ago when we were building roller coasters less than 150-feet tall? Now when you look at the best coasters in our nation and in the world, we are talking 450-to 500-feet in height. The sky is literally the limit, and the best is yet to come. In the coming few years, I am very confident that the next scream machine will be even taller, faster, and more surprising than we can ever imagine. Coasters like *X* show us that we can change the angle and perspective of the ride at every second. Flying coasters do indeed give a new perspective of what a coaster should look and feel like, and today's floorless coasters give the feel that we are sitting in our most comfortable easy chair while experiencing the action.

Also, with today's hydraulic launch coasters, we can now experience a zero to 130 mph cannon shot, like a fighter pilot going straight up to dizzying heights in **just seconds!** The true test of how fast and high we go will not rest in the limits of our imagination, but in how much stress and strain the human body can endure. When does a ride go over the boundaries of excitement and fun into an area where the rider has a clear potential of getting physically hurt from the attraction? That will be the key question in the minds of those who continue to build these mega marvels in the future.

Perhaps the next step will include an actual ride with the latest simulator technology that when combined together, create a new ride experience for all to enjoy. Who knows? But until we reach that point, I will still be looking forward to the next ride, the next rush, and the next gigantic roller coaster attraction to hit the market.

Listing of North American
Amusement Parks

United States

Alabama

Alabama Adventure (Visionland)- Bessemer, Alabama
Southern Adventures - Huntsville, Alabama
Waterville USA - Gulf Shores, Alabama

Arizona

Castles N' Corners - Phoenix, Arizona
Enchanted Island - Phoenix, Arizona
Funtasticks Family Fun Park - Tucson, Arizona

Arkansas

Magic Springs and Crystal Falls - Hot Springs, Arkansas

California

Adventure City - Stanton, California
Belmont Park - San Diego, California
Blackbeard's Family Fun Center - Fresno, California
California's Great America - Santa Clara, California
Disney's California Adventure - Anaheim, California

Disneyland - Anaheim, California
Funderwoods - Lodi, California
Gilroy Gardens Family Theme Park - Gilroy, California
Knott's Berry Farm - Buena Park, California
Legoland - Carlsbad, California
Nut Tree Family Park - Vacaville, California
Pacific Park - Santa Monica, California
Pixieland Park - Concord, California
Raging Waters - San Jose, California
Rotary Playland - Fresno, California
Santa Cruz Beach and Boardwalk - Santa Cruz, California
Sea World San Diego -San Diego, California
Six Flags Discovery Kingdom - Vallejo, California
Six Flags Magic Mountain - Valencia, California
Tahoe Amusement Park - South Lake Tahoe, California
Universal Studios Hollywood - Universal City, California

Colorado

Elitch Gardens - Denver, Colorado
Joyrides Family Fun Center - Colorado Springs, Colorado
Lakeside Amusement Park - Denver, Colorado
Santa's Workshop - North Pole, Colorado

Connecticut

Lake Compounce - Bristol, Connecticut
Quassy Amusement Park - Middlebury, Connecticut

Florida

Adventure Landing - Jacksonville Beach, Florida
Busch Gardens Africa -Tampa, Florida
Celebration Station - Clearwater, Florida
Cobra Adventure Park - Panama City Beach, Florida
Disney's Animal Kingdom - Lake Buena Vista, Florida
Disney's Hollywood Studio's - Lake Buena Vista, Florida
Disney's Magic Kingdom -Lake Buena Vista, Florida
EPCOT - Lake Buena Vista, Florida
King Richards's Family Fun Center- Naples, Florida
Old Town - Kissimmee, Florida
SeaWorld Orlando - Orlando, Florida
Universal Studio's Florida - Orlando, Florida
Universal's Islands of Adventure - Orlando, Florida
Wet and Wild Orlando - Orlando, Florida

Georgia

American Adventures- Marietta, Georgia
Funsville - Martinez, Georgia
Lake Winnepesaukah - Rossville, Georgia
Six Flags Over Georgia - Austell, Georgia
Wild Adventures - Valdosta, Georgia

Idaho

Silverwood Theme Park - Athol, Idaho

Illinois

Cherry Valley Golf and Games - Rockford, Illinois
Dinorex Arlington Heights - Arlington Heights, Illinois
Dinorex Crystal Lake - Crystal Lake, Illinois
Haunted Trails - Burbank, Illinois
Kiddieland - Melrose Park, Illinois
Safari Land - Villa Park, Illinois
Six Flags Great America - Gurnee, Illinois

Indiana

Fun Spot - Angola, Indiana
Holiday World and Spashin Safari - Santa Claus, Indiana
Indiana Beach - Monticello, Indiana

Iowa

Adventureland - Altoona, Iowa
Arnold's Park - Arnolds Park, Iowa

Kansas

All Star Adventures - Wichita, Kansas
Wild West World - Valley Center, Kansas

Kentucky

Beech Bend Park - Bowling Green, Kentucky
Six Flags Kentucky Kingdom - Louisville, Kentucky

Pete Trabucco

Louisiana

Carousel Gardens - New Orleans, Louisiana
Celebration Station - Baton Rouge, Louisiana
Dixie Landing - Baton Rouge, Louisiana
Hamel's Amusement Park - Shreveport, Louisiana

Maine

Funtown Splashtown - Saco, Maine
Palace Playland - Old Orchard Beach, Maine

Maryland

Adventure Park - New Market, Maryland
Baja Amusements - West Ocean City, Maryland
Jolly Roger Amusement Park - Ocean City, Maryland
Jolly Roger at the Pier - Ocean City, Maryland
Planet Fun - Greenbelt, Maryland
Six Flags America - Upper Marlboro, Maryland
Trimper's Rides - Ocean City, Maryland

Massachusetts

Six Flags New England - Agawam, Massachusetts

Michigan

Jeepers Great Lakes Crossing - Auburn Hills, Michigan
Jeepers Northland Mall - Southfield, Michigan
Michigan Adventure - Muskegon, Michigan

Minnesota

Como Town - St. Paul, Minnesota
Nickelodeon Universe - Bloomington, Minnesota
Paul Bunyan Land - Brainerd, Minnesota
Valleyfair - Shakopee, Minnesota

Missouri

Big Shot Amusement Park - Linn Creek, Missouri
Celebration City - Branson, Missouri
Miner Mike's Adventure Town - Osage Beach, Missouri
Route 66 Carousel Park - Joplin, Missouri
Silver Dollar City - Branson, Missouri
Six Flags St. Louis - Eureka, Missouri
Worlds of Fun - Kansas City, Missouri

Nebraska

Fun-Plex - Omaha, Nebraska
Scateland - Omaha, Nebraska

Nevada

Adventuredome - Las Vegas, Nevada
Buffalo Bill's Hotel and Casino - Jean, Nevada
Las Vegas Mini Gran Prix - Las Vegas, Nevada
NASCAR café - Las Vegas, Nevada
New York, New York Hotel and Casino - Las Vegas, Nevada
Playland Park - Reno, Nevada
Stratosphere Tower and Casino - Las Vegas, Nevada
Wild Island Family Adventure Park - Sparks, Nevada

New Hampshire

Canobie Lake - Salem, New Hampshire
Fun World - Nashua, New Hampshire
Santa's Village - Jefferson, New Hampshire
Six Gun City and Fort Splash - Jefferson, New Hampshire
Story Land - Glen, New Hampshire

New Jersey

Blackbeard's Cave - Bayville, New Jersey
Bowcraft Amusement Park - Scotch Plains, New Jersey
Casino Pier - Seaside Heights, New Jersey
Clementon Park and Splash World - Clementon, New Jersey
Fantasy Island - Beach Haven, New Jersey
Funtown Pier - Seaside Park, New Jersey
Gillian's Wonderland Pier - Ocean City, New Jersey
Jenkinson's Boardwalk - Point Pleasant Beach, New Jersey
Keansburg Amusement Park - Keansburg, New Jersey
Land of Make Believe - Hope, New Jersey
Morey's Pier's - Wildwood, New Jersey
Playland's Castaway Cove - Ocean City, New Jersey
Six Flags Great Adventure - Jackson, New Jersey
Steel Pier - Atlantic City, New Jersey
Storybook Land - Egg Harbor Township, New Jersey

New Mexico

Cliff's Amusement Park - Albuquerque, New Mexico
IT'Z - Albuquerque, New Mexico
Western Playland - Sunland Park, New Mexico

New York

Adventureland - Farmingdale, New York
Astroland - Brooklyn, New York
Boomers - Medford, New York
Coney Island Boardwalk - Brooklyn, New York
Coney island Bowery - Brooklyn, New York
Darien Lake - Darien Center, New York
Deno's Wonder Wheel Park - Brooklyn, New York
Hoffman's Playland - Latham, New York
Jeepers–Albany - Albany, New York
Kids N' Action - Brooklyn, New York
Krazy City - West Nyack, New York
Magic Forest - Lake George, New York
Martin's Fantasy Island - Grand Island, New York
Midway Park - Bemus Point, New York
Nellie Bly Amusement Park - Brooklyn, New York
Playland Park - Rye, New York
Seabreeze Amusement Park - Rochester, New York
Sports Plus - Lake Grove, New York
Sylvan Beach Amusement Park - Sylvan Beach, New York
The Great Escape and Splashwater Kingdom - Lake George, New York

North Carolina

Carowinds - Charlotte, North Carolina
Cherokee Fun Park - Cherokee, North Carolina
Ghost Town in the Sky - Maggie Valley, North Carolina
Santa's Land - Cherokee, North Carolina

Pete Trabucco

Ohio

Castaway Bay - Sandusky, Ohio
Cedar Point - Sandusky, Ohio
Coney Island - Cincinnati, Ohio
Geauga Lake and Whitewater Kingdom - Aurora, Ohio
Jungle Jack's Landing - Powell, Ohio
Kings Island - Mason, Ohio
Memphis Kiddy Park - Brooklyn, Ohio
Putt 'N Pond Speed Park - Fostoria, Ohio
Stricker's Grove - Ross, Ohio
Tuscora Park - New Philadelphia, Ohio
WonderPark - Cincinnati, Ohio

Oklahoma

Bartleville Kiddie Park - Bartlesville, Oklahoma
Celebration Station - Tulsa, Oklahoma
Frontier City - Oklahoma City, Oklahoma

Oregon

Enchanted Forrest - Turner, Oregon
Oaks Park - Portland, Oregon
Thrill-Ville USA - Turner, Oregon

Pennsylvania

Bushkill Park - Easton, Pennsylvania
DelGrosso's Amusement Park - Tipton, Pennsylvania
Dorney Park - Allentown, Pennsylvania
Dutch Wonderland - Lancaster, Pennsylvania
Hersheypark - Hershey, Pennsylvania
Idlewild and Soak Zone - Ligonier, Pennsylvania
Kennywood - West Mifflin, Pennsylvania
Knoebles Amusement Park - Elysburg, Pennsylvania
Lakemont Park - Altoona, Pennsylvania
Sesame Place - Langhorne, Pennsylvania
Waldameer Park - Erie, Pennsylvania

South Carolina

Family Kingdom Amusement Park - Myrtle Beach, South Carolina
Hard Rock Park - Myrtle Beach, South Carolina

Tennessee

Dollywood - Pigeon Forge, Tennessee
NASCAR Speed Park Sevierville, Tennessee
Sir Goony's Family Fun Center Chattanooga, Tennessee

Texas

Joyland Amusement Park - Lubbock, Texas
Kemah Boardwalk Amusements - Kemah, Texas
Kiddie Park - San Antonio, Texas
Oasis Lanes - El Paso, Texas
Schlitterbahn - New Braunfels, Texas
Sea World San Antonio - San Antonio, Texas
Six Flags Fiesta Texas - San Antonio, Texas
Six Flags Over Texas - Arlington, Texas
Wonderland Park - Amarillo, Texas
Zuma Fun Center - Houston, Texas

Utah

Lagoon - Farmington, Utah

Virginia

Busch Gardens–Europe - Williamsburg, Virginia
Kings Dominion - Doswell, Virginia
Motor World Virginia Beach - Virginia Beach, Virginia

Washington

Fun Forrest - Seattle, Washington
Puyallup Fair - Puyallup, Washington
Remlinger Farms - Carnation, Washington
Riverfront Park - Spokane, Washington
Wild Waves and Enchanted Village - Federal Way, Washington

West Virginia

Camden Park - Huntington, West Virginia

Wisconsin

Bay Beach - Green Bay, Wisconsin
Little A-Merrick-A - Marshall, Wisconsin
Noah's Ark - Wisconsin Dells, Wisconsin
Riverview Park and Waterworks - Wisconsin Dells, Wisconsin
Timber Falls Adventure Golf - Wisconsin Dells, Wisconsin

Canada

Atlantic Playland - Lower Fackville, Nova Scotia, Canada
Au Pays Des Marveilles - Sainte-Adèle, Québec, Canada
Burlington Amusement Park - Burlington, Prince Edward Island, Canada
Caloway Park, Calgary, Alberta, Canada
Canada's Wonderland - Maple, Ontario, Canada
Centreville Amusement Park - Toronto, Ontario, Canada
Chippewa Park - Thunder Bay, Ontario, Canada
Crystal Palace - Dieppe, New Brunswick, Canada
Galaxyland - Edmonton, Alberta, Canada
Kingston Family Fun World - Kingston, Ontario, Canada
La Ronde - Montréal, Québec, Canada
Marineland - Niagara Falls, Ontario, Canada
Playland - Vancouver, British Columbia, Canada
Sandspit - Hunter River, Prince Edward Island, Canada
Santa's Village - Bracebridge, Ontario, Canada
Geauga Lake and Whitewater Tinkertown - Winnipeg, Manitoba, Canada
Upper Clements Park - Annapolis Royal, Nova Scotia, Canada
Wild Zone Adventures - Chatham, Ontario, Canada

Roller Coaster Terminology

A

Acceleration-Describes when the coaster's cars or trains are gaining speed. The term is most commonly used to describe how fast a train reaches a specific speed particularly on a launch coaster.

Airtime-Term used to describe the feeling created by negative-g forces. Airtime is the sensation of floating while riding a roller coaster when your body is forced up from the seat creating air between the seat and your bottom. Airtime or negative-g forces are most commonly experienced on a drop or at the crest of a hill.

Anti-Rollback Device-A ratcheting device used on a lift hill or section of a roller coaster that prevents the cars or trains from rolling backward. That familiar clicking sound you hear on the track on the lift hill up the coaster is this device in action.

Ascend-To rise up a hill, tower, or any incline in the course of a ride.

B

Backward Riding-This term refers to riding a roller coaster while seated facing in the opposite direction you are traveling. Amusement parks will on occasion run a roller coaster backward by placing the train backward on the track so the rear car goes down the hill first. On shuttle coasters (Vekoma is a good example) riders will travel backward and forward since the roller coaster track does not form a complete circuit.

Banked Turn-Describes a section of track that is banked (laterally angled) while turning. Designers bank the turns on roller coasters to reduce the lateral g-forces inside the train.

Barrel Roll-An inversion term that basically is a corkscrew maneuver on a roller coaster. See corkscrew.

Bench Seats-A flat-seat designed with no divider between the riders. Bench seats were common on older wooden coasters and mine train coasters. A bench seat allows riders to slide across the seat. Today, most coasters are designed for more safety and security and have seat dividers or bucket seats to meet modern safety specifications.

Boomerang-A type of inversion with two half loops connected to each other. Boomerang is also the term used by Vekoma to describe one of their shuttle coaster models. A similar maneuver would also be called a cobra roll.

Brake Run-A section of track usually before the loading station where brakes are installed to bring the incoming trains to a complete stop. Brake runs may also be installed midway through the course to slow a car down and decrease replacement of the wheels for that train.

Brakes-basically used to slow or stop the train on a roller coaster. Brakes are placed on the brake run, but may also be located along the course the train travels to slow the train down if necessary or stop it. Brakes can be physical in nature or can use magnetic forces to stop or slow down a train.

C

Camel Back-A series of hills on a steel or wooden roller coaster where each preceding one is slightly smaller then the proceeding one. Camel backs produce negative g's or "air time."

Car-A car is a part of the overall coaster train. A car consists of one or more rows where riders are seated in individual or bench seats. A coaster train should consist of two or more cars linked together to form the train.

Catapult Launch-The coaster train is launched to give it power instead of using a lift hill and gravity. The catapult system connects with the train and accelerates the train using a flywheel or weight drop. More recently, compressed-air (thrust air), Linear Synchronous Motors (LSM's) and Linear Induction Motors (LIM's) are being used as well to launch a train.

Chain Lift-The chain lift is one of the fundamental elements of most roller coasters. The chain lift pulls the car or train to the top of a hill and then releases the train to coast down a hill where gravity takes effect and the train accelerates down the course. On some coasters more than one lift hill may be used.

Circuit-Used to describe a complete roller coaster track from start to finish.

Cobra Roll-A term describing a signature element on some roller coasters designed by Bolliger and Mabillard. The cobra roll is a double inversion similar to a boomerang element. Riders enter the element and are sent upside down twice and leaving going in the opposite direction they were as they entered.

Corkscrew-A corkscrew is a twisting inversion designed like a corkscrew. Arrow Dynamics designed the world's first corkscrew inversion. Barrel roll is the term used by Bolliger and Mabillard to describe their corkscrew inversion.

Pete Trabucco

D

Diving Loop-A term used to describe an inversion similar to an acrobatic stunt plan maneuver. This inversion involves half a vertical loop and a twisting curve leading either in or out of the inversion. On the B & M inverted coasters, this inversion is also referred to as an Immelman.

Double Dip-A hill that has been divided into two separate drops by a flattening out of the drop midway down the hill. The Jack Rabbit at Kennywood is one of the most famous coasters that utilize this maneuver and still running today.

Double Loop-A term used to describe an element of two vertical loops together or may be used to describe a roller coaster with two vertical inversions, and no other inversions.

Double Out and Back-A term used to describe the layout on a roller coaster where the track heads away and returns to the station twice. See related terms: out and back, triple out and back.

Dual Track-The term used to describe a roller coaster with two different tracks or circuits. A dual track coaster shares the station and may share some parts of the structure including the lift hill.

Dueling Coaster-A dual track roller coaster that is designed to produce the effect of near, head-on collisions through the circuit. Dueling Dragons at Universals Studio's Islands of Adventure is a classic example of this type of coaster.

E

Enclosed-A roller coaster where the entire track is housed inside a building or some sort of structure. Theme parks generally build coasters inside a structure so they may theme the ride with lighting, sound, or other special effects.

F

Figure Eight Layout-A roller coaster track layout that resembles the number eight from above.

First Drop-The first major drop on a roller coaster and generally the first drop following the lift hill.

Fixed Lapbar-A restraint on a coaster train that a rider sits under that locks in a designated position and does not adjust. Because of an increase in safety awareness fixed lab bar (for each individual) restraints are replacing full train restraints.

Flat Spin-A term used by coaster designers to describe their banked, high-speed helix turns.

Flat Turn-A turn where the track remains flat and gives the sensation that the train my tip due to the lateral forces. Most turns on a coaster are banked, but in some cases, a flat turn may be used to increase the thrills. *The Cyclone* in Coney Island, New York is a good example of utilizing these flat turns.

G

G-Force–The Amount of gravitation force that is put on the body. For example, two g's would equal twice the force of gravity on your body. If you weight two hundred pounds in a two g maneuver, you will be carrying four hundred pounds on your body at this time.

Gigacoaster-A marketing term used by Cedar Point and manufacturer Intamin to describe a roller coaster that stands more than three hundred feet tall. Millennium Force a 310-feet high.

H

Heartline-A term used to describe an inversion where the center of gravity is designed around the rider's heart line.

Helix-A turn on a roller coaster course that forms a radius of more than 360-degrees.

Hypercoaster-A term used to describe a steel roller coaster designed for speed and airtime. Hypercoasters have large drops for speed, have no inversions and have plenty of camelbacks, bunny hops, or speed bumps for airtime.

I

Immelman-A term used to describe their diving loop on inverted roller coasters. This element was named for an airplane maneuver invented by a German pilot in World War II.

Indoor Roller Coaster-An indoor roller coaster operates inside a building, such as an indoor amusement park, mall, or other venue. They can also be dark rides such as *Space Mountain* located at both Disney Land and Disney World parks.

Inversion-A term used to describe any portion of a roller coaster track that turns the riders upside down.

Inverted Roller Coaster-A roller coaster with trains suspended beneath the track above.

J

Junior Coaster-A term also used to describe a kiddie-coaster or a simple roller coaster designed especially for children and frightened parents.

L

Lapbar-A type of restraint that secures the rider by placing a bar across the passengers lap. A lapbar restraint can be designed to secure an individual rider or multiple riders.

Lifthill-The section of the coaster that contains some device or mechanism that pulls or pushes the roller coaster train up a hill. The majority of lifthills use a chain connected to a motor that

Pete Trabucco

pulls the train to the top. Some roller coasters contain multiple lifthills and the lifthill may be midcourse or at the end of the circuit.

Linear Induction Motor (LIM)-A magnetic motor commonly used to launch a roller coaster train along or up a section of steel track. LSM or Linear Synchronous Motors are the same idea, but the technology used to propel the train is different.

Looping Corkscrew or Loop Screw-A type of roller coaster that features a vertical loop and a corkscrew.

Loading Platform-The part of the station where the riders board the roller coaster train.

M

Manual Brake-A hand operated brake requiring a human to operate that slows or stops a roller coaster train. Many classic wooden roller coasters have manual brake systems, but in recent years, they're becoming rare as parks replace the manual brakes with computerized brake systems. *The Cyclone* in Coney Island, New York still operates this way.

Mine Train-A genre of early steel roller coasters with a layout that features fast, quick turns, drops, and helix turns. Most are themed after a runaway mine train. One of the first of these appeared at Six Flags Over Texas in Arlington, Texas.

N

Negative G's-Negative g's generate airtime or the sensation of floating while on a roller coaster. Negative G's are usually found on a roller coaster at the top of a hill when the rider's body is accelerated upwards. These types of g-forces are more uncomfortable to riders than positive g-forces that press you into your seat.

O

Out and Back-A term used to describe a type of layout on a roller coaster. An out and back roller coaster layout is where the train leaves the station and heads out to a point where there is a turnaround to send the train back to the station. Sometimes variations can be found like an L-layout out and back where the turnaround is not the only curve in the roller coaster. Some out and back coasters like *Shivering Timbers* at Michigan's Adventure will have a helix at the end of the layout, but still maintain a correct out and back layout.

Over-The-Shoulder Restraint (OTSR)-A device that goes over the riders shoulders to restrain and protect them while riding a roller coaster. Another name for these type of restraints are horse collars.

P

Partially Enclosed-A roller coaster where only a portion of the track is within an enclosed structure or building.

Pay-One-Price-Amusement Park admission structure where you pay-one-price for all rides, shows, and attractions and is often called a POP ticket. The other option if available is to pay-as-you-go, in which case you would use tickets for the rides, attractions, and shows. Disney Theme Parks are examples of POP admission parks, and Knoebels Amusement Park is an example of a park that has POP as an option on selected days, but always offers the option to pay-as-you-go.

Positive G's-Gravitational forces that pull you downward that are often found in inversions, highly banked, high speed turns and at the bottom of hills. Positive G-forces are when the gravitational force exceeds one g, giving you the sensation of feeling heavier than you actually are.

R

Racer-A dual track roller coaster designed where the trains leave the station at the same moment and race each other through the circuit. Most racing coasters like *Colossus* at Six Flags Magic Mountain feature parallel tracks. Other coasters like *Rolling Thunder* at Six Flags Great Adventure or *Lightning Racer* at Hershey Park race, but each track is entirely different.

Restraint-Some sort of device to prevent the rider from leaving the roller coaster train while it's in motion. The fundamental idea of the restraint is to protect the rider and keep them in the proper riding position throughout the duration of the ride. Commonly found restraints include lap bars, over-the-shoulder restraints, and seat belts.

Running Rails-A term used to describe the track or rails the train or car on a roller coaster rides on.

S

Seats-The location where the rider sits in the car or train while riding the roller coaster.

Seatbelt-A rather simple device used to help restrain and protect the rider. On some roller coasters like the *Matterhorn* at Disneyland this is the only restraint device, but on many other coasters seat belts are being used in addition to another restraint like a lap bar.

Shoulder Harness-A device used to secure a rider's shoulders by placing a bar over the shoulder area, but unlike an over-the-shoulder restraint it does not go down over the chest, stomach, and cross the riders lap. Also see Over-The-Shoulder Restraint.

Shuttle-A term used to describe a roller coaster track that does not form a complete circuit. Instead the train or car is required to traverse the track in one direction and then reverse directions and return by repeating the course over again going in the opposite

Pete Trabucco

direction. *The Boomerang* at Morey's Pier in Wildwood, New Jersey is a good example of a shuttle coaster.

Side Friction-A roller coaster designed with guide rails above and on the outside of the track or running rails. The guide rails keep the train or car on the track without the use of guide wheels or upstops. *Leap the Dips* (the oldest operational coaster in the world) at Lakemont Park is an example of a side friction roller coaster.

Single Loop-A roller coaster layout that only contains one, vertical loop. *California Screaming* at Disneyland's California Adventure in Anaheim, California is the best example of this type of ride.

Speed Bump-A small hill placed in a location where it will be taken at a high speed and will produce negative g-forces or airtime lifting the riders out of their seats.

Spinning Wild Mouse-A Wild Mouse coaster designed with cars that spin during the entire course or parts of the roller coaster. The spinning is not controlled by mechanics, but instead by gravity, weight distribution, and other forces caused by the ride.

Stand-Up Roller Coaster-A roller coaster design that permits the riders to stand during the entire ride instead of being seated. This is not a ride for someone with bad knees!

Station-The station is a building or structure that houses the loading and unloading platforms for a roller coaster. The station may also contain the ride's control panel, maintenance shed and a train storage area or transfer track.

Steel Roller Coaster-A roller coaster built with steel rails as opposed to an all wood construction.

Suspended-A roller coaster designed where the trains ride below the track rather than on top of the track. *The Arrow Suspended like Big Bad Wolf* at Busch Gardens Williamsburg have special trains that are designed to swing freely from side to side.

Suspended Looping Coaster (SLC)-A term used by Vekoma to describe its inverted roller coaster design.

T

Terrain Roller Coaster-A term used to describe a roller coaster layout that makes use of the terrain and natural surroundings. The coaster track is generally kept low to the ground and the surrounding terrain generally adds to the ride experience. A good example of this is *Boulder Dash* at Lake Compounce in Bristol, Connecticut.

Theme Park-A term used to describe an amusement park that is designed to carry a theme in one or more areas of the park. The theme may carry over to the rides and attractions in that area as well. Examples of theme parks include Holiday World, Islands of Adventure, Disneyland, Magic Kingdom, and Knott's Berry Farm.

Traditional Amusement Park-A term used to describe an amusement park that continues to operate in a manner similar

California Screaming at Disneyland's California Adventure in Anaheim, California

Pete Trabucco

California Screaming at Disneyland's California Adventure in Anaheim, California

to the way parks operated in the early 1900's. Examples include Kennywood, Knoebels Amusement Resort, Lake Compounce, and Playland Park in Rye, New York.

Train-A group of one or more cars linked together to form a roller coaster train.

Turnaround-A term that describes a turn on a roller coaster that sends the train back going in the opposite direction it came from. Turnarounds are common on roller coasters with an out and back layout.

Twister-Describes a roller coaster layout that features many turns, crossovers, and track that runs in many directions. A twister is a roller coaster layout that is unpredictable. Examples include *Roar* at Six Flags Marine World, *Cyclone* at Astroland, and the *Wildcat* at Hershey Park.

Two Lift Hills-A roller coaster that includes two lift hills.

U

Unloading Platform-The part of the station where the passengers unload from the train or car. On many roller coasters the loading and unloading platform is the same thing.

Upstops-A part of a train that is generally a flat piece of steel with a nylon or rubber surface that is attached to the train and placed underneath the track or to keep the train from flying off. If the upstop comes in contact with the track due to the train rising from negative g-forces it will slide along the track and prevent the train from rising any further.

V

Vertical Loop-A term used to describe an inversion that is a 360-degree loop placed in a vertical position where riders are sent upside down once.

W

Weight Drop Launch-Found on some versions of the Schwarzkopf shuttle loop roller coasters. The weight drop launch uses a large weight attached by steel cables to pulleys that when released pulls the train from the station, accelerating it to its top speed.

Wheels-Describes the part of the roller coaster car or train that rolls on the rails or track. Wheels are typically steel with a nylon or rubber coating on the outside to reduce the noise steel to steel contact would make and the heat generated by friction. There are three types of wheels on a roller coaster. Also see Guide Wheel, Road Wheel, and Upstop Wheel.

Wild Mouse-A term that describes a type of roller coaster with sharp turns that are not banked and quick steep drops. Wild Mouse coasters typically run with two or four passenger individual cars as opposed to trains.

Wooden Structure-Describes the support structure of a roller coaster that is made out of wood.

Wooden Roller Coaster-A roller coaster that uses layers of laminated wood with a flat steel rail attached to the top and inside as the track.

Pete
Trabucco

Pete has been an avid pilot and roller coaster enthusiast for the past 10 years. He has traveled all over the country and has ridden over three hundred roller coasters in this time period. Pete continues to work as a *Sales Manager* in the aviation industry and has done so since 1998. He has worked for several Fortune 500 companies including BP Corporation based out of Manchester, England.

Pete has also been involved with the American Heart Association serving as Director of Regional Sales and Training for AHA in the state of New Jersey.

His responsibilities at AHA included the management and growth of the New Jersey hospital resuscitation-training network, which consisted of a fifty-five hospital and 5,500-instructor member program. He also helped this organization by successfully lobbying for several health bills at the statehouse including the Automated External Defibrillation PAD (Public Access Defibrillation) bill. This legislation would eventually become the model that would be utilized by all fifty states and was signed into law on the federal level in 1999.

A graduate of Kean University, Pete worked several years as New Jersey State Assembly Chief of Staff in the nineteenth and thirty-fourth New Jersey legislative districts. He is currently a major in the US Air Force Auxiliary New Jersey Wing Civil Air Patrol (CAP) program based out of McGuire Air Force Base in Wrightstown, New Jersey. He has been involved with this organization since 1987 and has held the position of *Central Jersey Squadron*

Commander and *223 Deputy Group Commander* for the New Jersey wing. Pete received his pilot's certification in 1991 and has been twice awarded the Air Force Chief of Staff award at the Pentagon for his work with this organization. He enjoys committing his time toward helping his community, state, and nation and he truly enjoys being involved in public service.

Finally, Pete has written and has published dozens of national articles in the fields of aviation, healthcare and politics. He is constantly asked to speak at conferences and seminars on these topics. Pete is married and has a daughter named Jennifer.